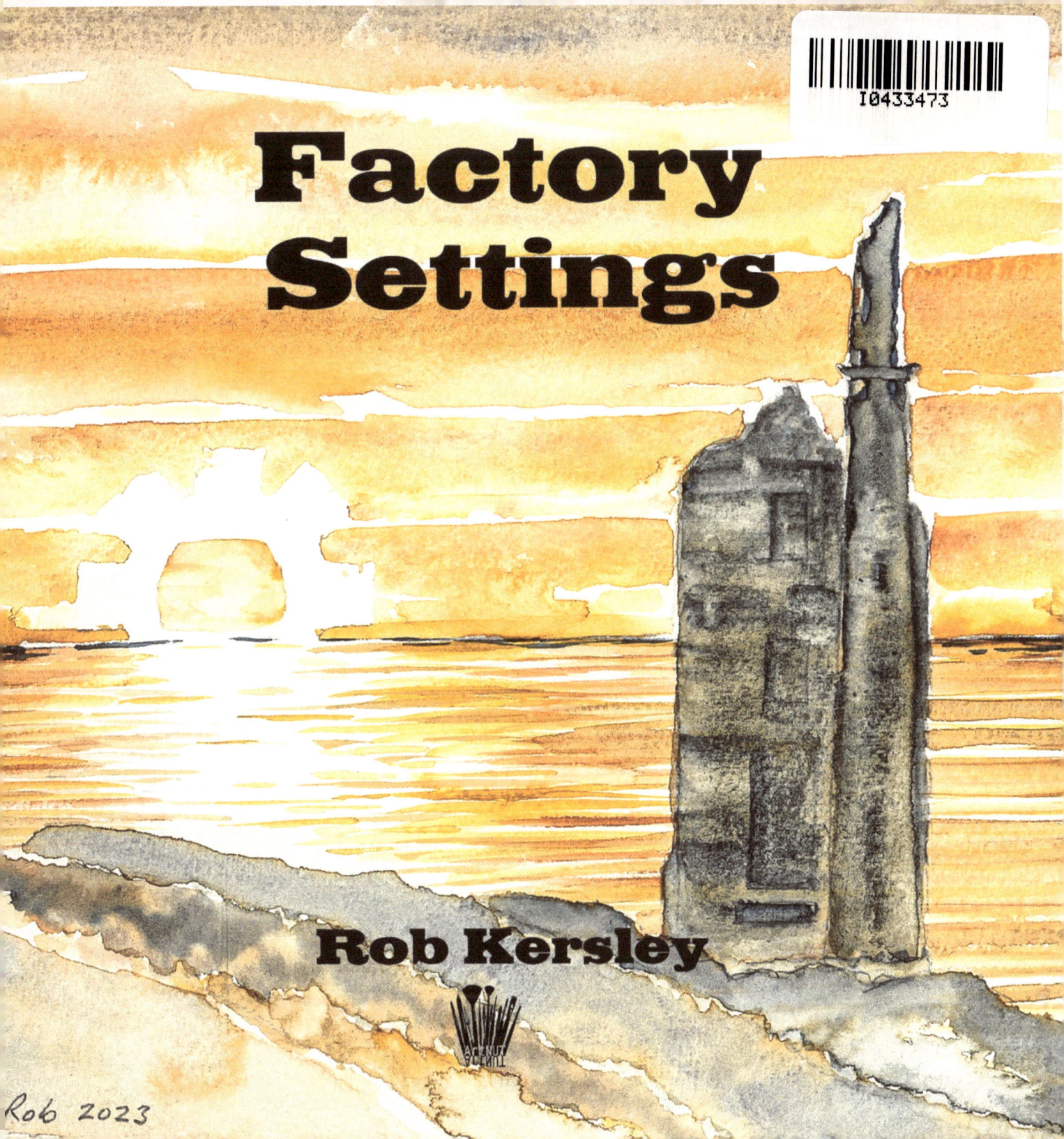

Rob Kersley

Copyright © Rob Kersley 2023

The right of Rob Kersley to be identified as the author of this work has been asserted in accordance with sections 77 and 78 of the Copyright Design and Patent Act 1988.

Email: rlkersley@aol.co.uk

Published by ArtNut imprint of MA Publisher (Penzance)
Email: mapublisher@yahoo.com
Website: www.mapublisher.org.uk
Released on November 2023

Print on Demand books are printed in each region of the continent listed and distributed there through the print on demand chain.
Australia | Canada | Europe | UK | USA

ISBN-13: 978-1-915958-04-4

All rights reserved. No part of this publication may be reproduced, stored in a retrieval system, or transmitted, in any form or by any means, electronic, mechanical, photocopying, recording, public performances or otherwise, without prior written permission of the copyright holder, except for brief quotations embodied in critical articles or reviews.

Disclaimer:
All expressions and opinions of the work belong to the artists/Author and MAP & ArtNut does not share or endorse any other than to provide the open platform to publish their work. For further information on MAP policies please email: mapublisher@yahoo.com for further information and submission guidelines.

Cover designed by Mayar Akash
Cover image: by Rob Kersley (Penzance, Cornwall)
Copy edit: Liz Kersley
Typeset in Times Roman, Title font: Cairo SF

Paper printed on is FSC Certified, lead free, acid free, buffered paper made from wood-based pulp. Our paper meets the ISO 9706 standard for permanent paper. As such, paper will last several hundred years when stored.

Dedication

For the victims, the also rans, the evicted and the displaced.

Acknowledgements

Thank you once again to Mayar Akash. Probably the most supportive, diligent and patient publisher on the planet and without whom, none of these poems would have seen the light of day.

To Michelle Blaken, who photographed my watercolours and seemed to raise the bar even higher in this second book.

To my friends and family who now extend around this extraordinary planet, and to whom I only have to reach out, to know that there are still so many things to celebrate, to protest against and to marvel at, and whose love makes that work both essential and possible.

And to my rock, my wife Liz. This book is as much yours as it is mine.

Contents

Dedication	3
Acknowledgements	4
Introduction	7
This Thing Called Marriage.	9
The First Page	11
Now Wash Your Hands	13
A Lull In Lithuania	15
Planet Tyson	19
Between The Tides	23
Au Revoir	25
Our Ken	27
Together	29
Windsor Barbie	33
Minder	35
A Clean Sheet	39
Swallows	41
Dismount In Ferragudo	44
Beneath The Same Sky	46
Stay Safe	53
Tips On Cutting Your Wife's Hair	56
Impossiblethornectomy	58
Begging For An Encore	60
Bird Whisperer	63
When We Go Back	64
Don't Stare Into The Sun	67
Hush Little Baby	68
No Harp, No Wings	69
No Price Tag	71
Pain Of Life	75
She	78
The Brits Are Coming!	79
Acknowledge	83
Accept	84
Evolve	87
Just Tell Me The Truth	89
Feeling Thrown	91
Homeward With Em' Spoonerisms	93
Prime Location, Christmas Eve	95
Nellie The President	97
Look Inside	99

Ten	101
The England Machine	103
About The Author	104

Introduction

I am delighted to introduce my second book. As with my first book, *Time and Tide*, these poems are sequenced in chronological order, just as they first appeared under the heading of Honddu Valley Herald.

The starting point then, was the summer of 2019 and the run up to my daughter Kath's wedding. The thirty-nine pieces then cover that very wedding; losing our dear Labrador Woody; an epic road trip through eastern Europe and Scandinavia; and finally, travelling to Portugal for what should have been a couple of months in the sun but which unfolded into practically the entire year as the pandemic and its travel restrictions came to bear with the resulting, unexpected feelings of homesickness and a longing for some normality, before our eventual return home to West Cornwall.

As if that wasn't enough, within that strange period there was also a U.K. general election, Donald Trump lost his job and I was persuaded to cut my wife's hair! All these experiences are covered in this book. However, the underlying backdrop was one of increased restrictions, isolation and a total absence of clarity whilst all the while clinging on to one enormous positive: that when this jarring disorder was finally over, our new normal would carry within it a resetting of our values to more fundamental thinking; the appreciation of care-workers, the clapping of the N.H.S. the looking out for neighbours, and the acceptance and respect of the overwhelming forces of nature, and that this would leave us more considerate, more careful, more caring, and more appreciative of others goodwill too, a kind of cleansing and returning to our original factory settings.

In hindsight, this ideology now seems over-simplistic and somewhat naive; but it could also be the case that over time our factory settings have themselves shifted, and that what we have now defaulted to (post pandemic), really is our new basic platform, our current reconfigured processing format, our nuanced contemporary styling, and our very best reinvention. These are the underlying questions posed in Factory Settings.

I sincerely thank you for your support and very much hope that you enjoy this collection.

Give me just one day
of this love
To find all the answers
I ever sought.

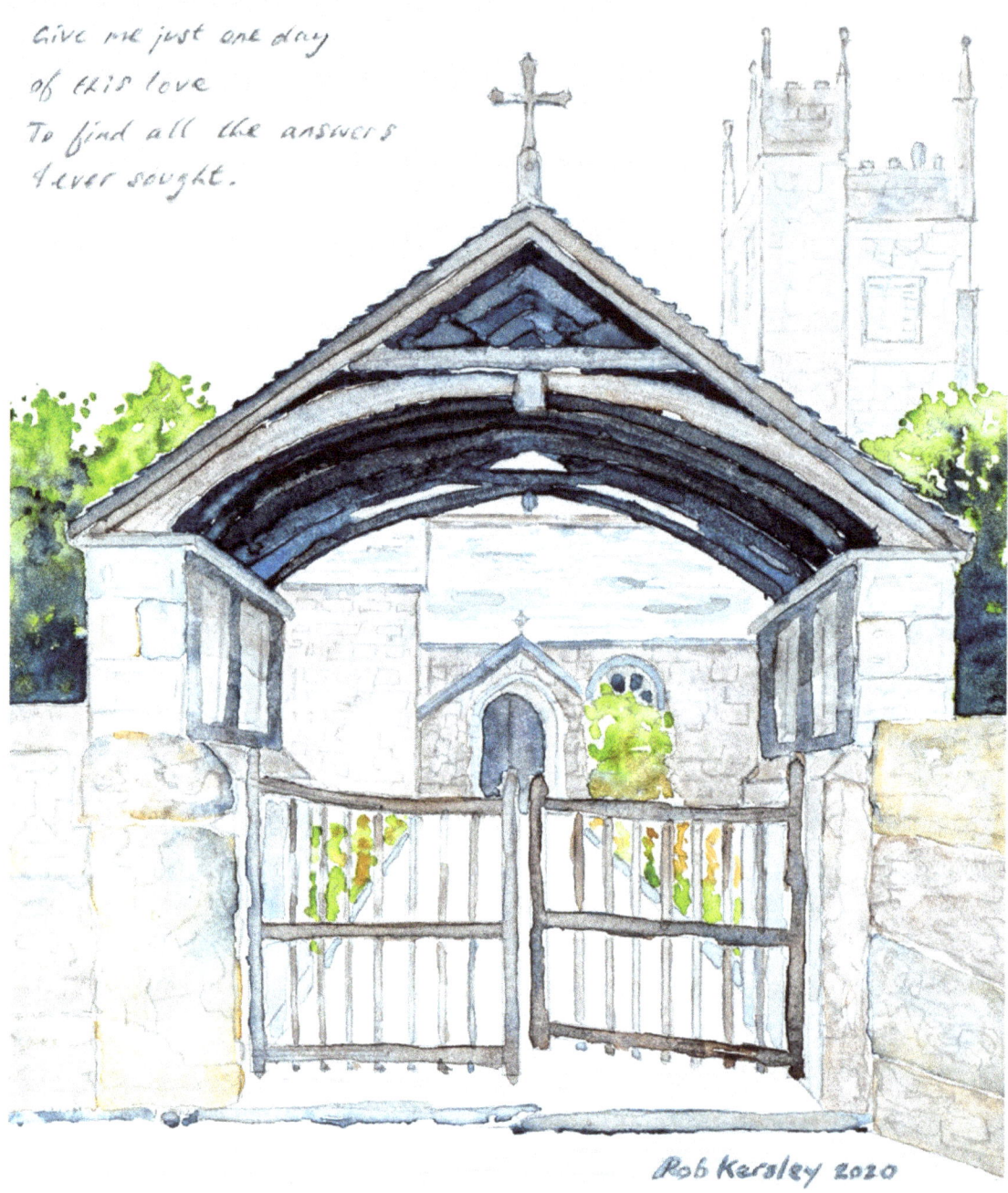

This Thing Called Marriage.

To Kath and John, just seven days before your journey begins.

Hold her in your arms.
Hold her so close that she can't fail
To feel what it means.
Hold her so close that she knows
That the seas could freeze
That the mountains could erupt
And the skies could fill with fire
And you would still be there
That your love would never fail.

Kiss him on the lips,
Kiss him with your heart.
Close your eyes and give everything of yourself,
Everything you were
Everything you will be.
Every day, every night,
Every thought, every deed.
Through your laughter, amid your tears.
All that you see,
And all he hears.

Give me just one day of this love
To find all the answers I ever sought.
I'll take one mile of this journey,
Where the certainty of two hearts that beat in time.
Means that nothing matters
But the knowing that you truly love.
Not the head-spinning infatuation
Nor the glimmer of a promise.
Not the compromise of some negotiation,
But the commitment of everything,
The sum of every part and more.
Not just the flesh but the bones
Not just the heart, but the soul.
The knowing that you both belong
The knowing that you've found each other.
That everything else, you can do without,
And the certainty
That this love
Is all you'll ever need.

God bless you both,
Dad. x

Rob Kersley

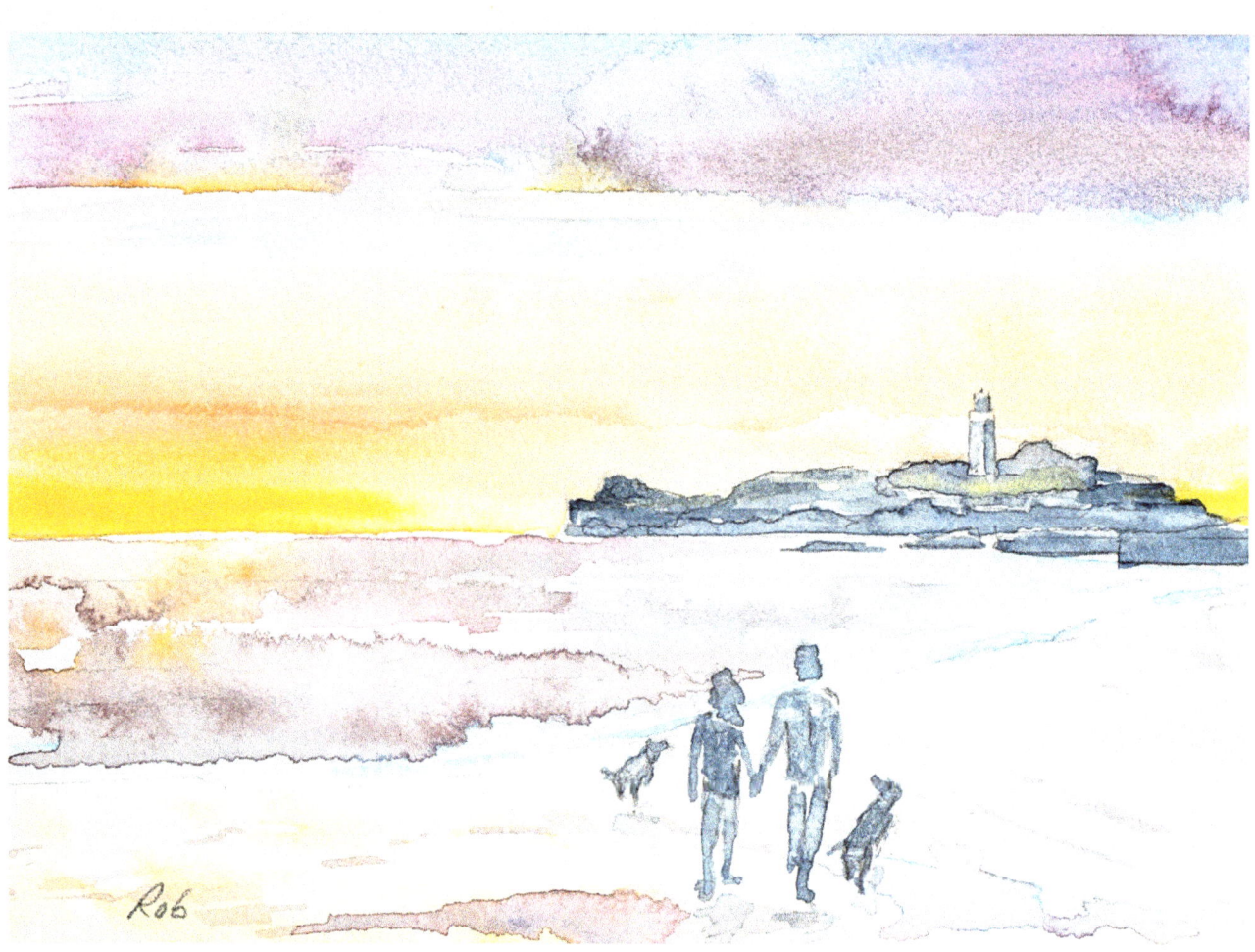

The First Page

    The day arose from behind the eastern hills of Godolphin.

...Their chosen day,
Revealed at last
As the heavy curtain of dawn
Was slowly hoisted,
Above the broadening grin of low early morning light
Stretching itself over the Penwith hedges,
Its sharpening fingers of shortening shadows
Looked beyond the saffron hamlets,
To find her in Penponds.

They blew a warm, honey dew breeze,
That crept through the open sash window,
Brushed gently across her pillow
And kissed her awake.

They had gathered.
Peeping over each other's shoulders,
All those who had had their time,
All those from whom she came.
In a murmuring, nodding, smiling, approving, huddle.
Gathering around the corners,
Peering back through the mirrors.
White lace and eucalyptus,
Those finishing touches,
The diminishing blushes
Of a girl,
To this finished work
Of perfect womanhood before them.

They swept past, overhead
To Gwinnear
And held their collective breath
Swallowing hard as the bells peeled
And hands, trembling with the power of this thing within
Were gently bound
As their eyes locked
Their souls, immortally,
Indelibly docked.   cont.

They swept down
And grasped at the fluttering confetti
Before dashing away,
To take their places amid the poms poms,
The Prosecco,
The pure white table cloths
And the fairy lights,
To hear the speeches and the toasts.
Until they nudged the Welsh cakes
Ever closer to the guests
Giggling with anticipation
At the potent contents
Alchemy, in perfect disguise.

Their chemistry devised:
Cakes of Cymru,
Pasties from the Duchy,
Those Sandy Acre Seven,
And a sudden, untamable
Release of coiled tension.
That saw trousers split open
And kindred spirits sky high,
Demanding
Johnny Be Good
To Miss American Pie.

The biggest, fattest, Celtic wedding
That came in on a spring tide of love.
Salty, smiling eyes gazed down from above
Until the landmark day slipped quietly westward over Trink.

They craned to get one last look
At the final flickering images of so many perfect chapters
Where, in spite of everything in a contradictory world,
True love still survives.
And the outstretched opening pages
Of a new,
Unwritten book.

The very first day,
Of the rest of their lives.

Now Wash Your Hands

Shoulder to shoulder at the supermarket urinals,
He finished before me,
Zipped himself up,
Checked himself out in the mirror,
Ignored the sign:
"Now wash your hands",
Left a considerate, glazed hand print on the door handle,
And re-joined the shoppers.

A minute later,
After scrubbing obsessively
I waited for the door to be swung open.
And sneaked through
To avoid contamination.

There he stood, reading a tabloid
He was never going to buy.
Upright, well-fed,
Well-heeled, scanning the columns,
Not so well-read.

So casually, he skipped over the headlines,
Looking for something to spice up his day.
Schools contemplating a four day week to try to balance the books,
He doesn't have young children.
Windrush victims still waiting for their promised payment,
He's not black.
NHS on a shoe string,
He's not on a ward.
Social care in near collapse,
He doesn't give it a thought.
Dangerously low police numbers,
His area's alright.
Diminishing public transport,
His pride is his gleaming steed.
Steel factories are closing,
His pension's guaranteed.

I will not cease from mental fight, disgraced
When Clarkson and Katy Hopkins replaced,

cont.

Rob Kersley

Empathy, sterilized without a trace,
A pogrom of progress, lost in space.
His Jerusalem now, he cuts and pastes.
Vacuum packed, sanitized of taste.
This chipboard snob, devoid of grace,
His green and pleasant land, laid waste.

At last, something grabs his attention;
Both candidates are promising further tax cuts
(that they know we can't afford).

There you go
...Re-fold the paper,
Put it back on the news stands.
Glance at the world from a safe distance
...Now wash your hands.

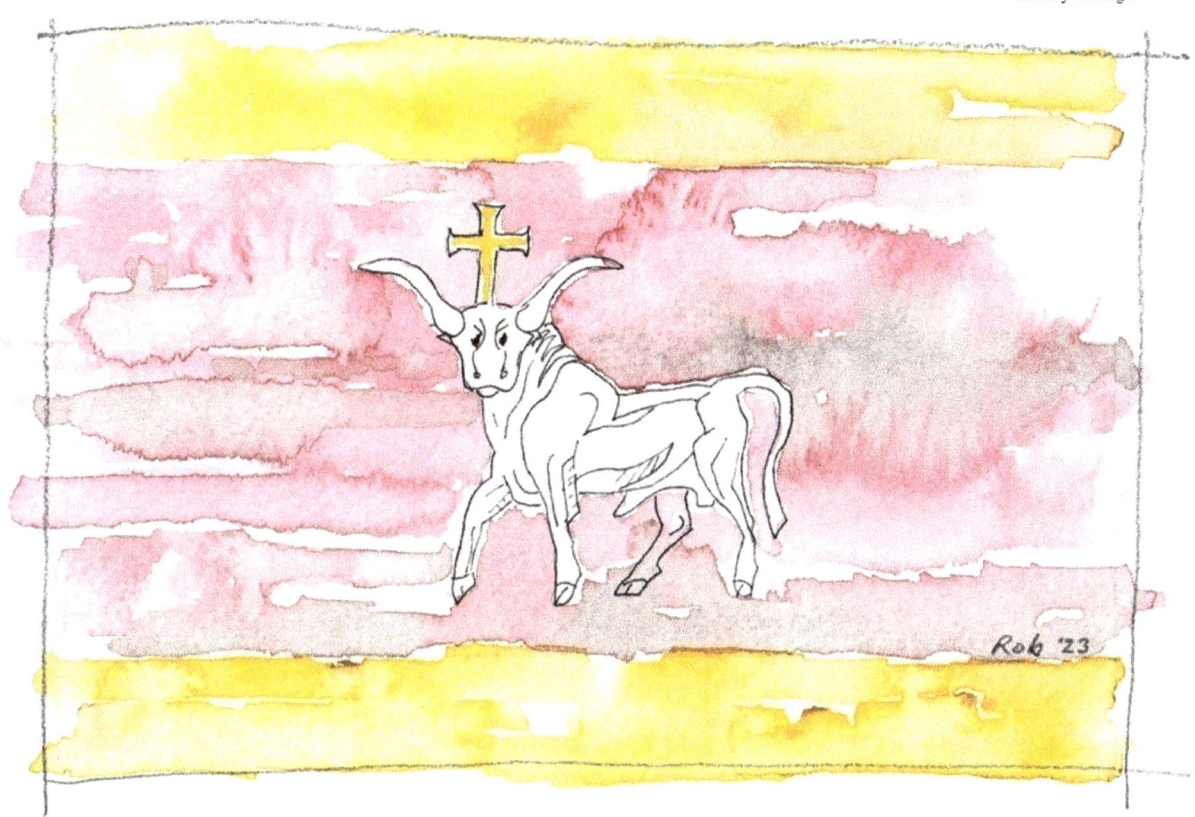

A Lull in Lithuania

A lull in Lithuania...
Nothing on the telly for the family in Kaunas,
Lithuania's Got Talent has finished,
And, *A Lyga* has yet to begin.
So they dip once more
Into the slowly unfolding soap,
The full series box set, enthralled in us.
To the terracotta streets
Of Vilnius.

Something stimulating in the slow-mo collapse,
Something sagacious in observing such a public fall from grace.
Something sad but satisfying,
When at long, long last they're on their way up,   cont.

And they crane their collectively concerned crowns.
Bite, to steady a trembling lip as they recall darker days.
Hands held in unity, so badly burned,
Like a vigil held to mistakes so painlessly made
From which they are agonizingly learned.
And pity
The embarrassed, befuddled, fools on their way down.

Nothing on TV in the Nederlands.
Voice of Holland has ended,
And *Eredivisie* has yet to start.
But the news is full at least.
Reality TV,
Real life.
Real UK life,
And a binge-watching Dutch public make themselves comfortable
As British leaders tie themselves up in transparent knots.
Like vipers, fighting to get out of a toxic pit.
Clammy, slimy slithering,
Spineless invertebrates
Crawling over and under, looking for a plausible escape,
Then pulled back into the trench,
Suffocating in the cynical septic stench
Of lies, on top of lies, on top of lies.
...As Dutch families
On neat Dutch sofas
In neat Dutch towns,
Watch from the neat, Dutch safety
Of their neat, Dutch sensibility.

What do Germans think of the side show.
Even better than
Mieten, Kaufen, Wohnen.
More entertaining than the *Bundersliga.*
Yes, the British slide,
Yes, that flag waving, British pride.
That came long before, the British fall.
No tabloid sympathy for Tommy,
And his spectacular demise.
Those aren't tears of sadness,
De Bild laughs so much, it cries.

And those news stands in Helsinki,   cont.

The headlines:
Farce,
Comedy,
Johnson,
Brexit.
Back-stop.
What do they want ... a Border? No Border?
A deal? No deal?
Out, but still In?
In, and yet Out?

The grubby side of the EU has nothing on us.
Even the screwed-up, crumpled fag packets
Still life on beer-sloshed sticky bar tables on a still, Sunday morning,
That line the pavements of Arkadiankatu.
Yes, folk can be stupid here too,
Metro traders
Assured, no-brainers
In retro trainers
More paranoid about not looking cool,
Than of the tragic images of death and the dying on those very packets
At twenty euros a throw.
Twenty euros up in smoke.
Twenty drags,
Twenty shorts
And twenty more
For twenty wards.

But stupidity, Helsinki style,
Can't begin to compare with
The staggering along the very edge.
Helsinki isn't sleep-walking out, onto the wind swept ledge
Hanover isn't tearing itself to shreds
Eindhoven isn't unravelling its trusted threads.
And Kaunas,
Beautiful Kaunas knows, only too well,
There are some things, with which you just don't meddle.

A woman at a café near Stockholm.
Hears me speak in my Cymru-fied, English tongue
Looks at me with a mixture
Of pity, disgust and stupefied confusion.
Us, Westerners: cont.

Us, the subjects of Trump and Johnson,
Us, the problem, the anti-solution.

Just what would it take for us
To lay down in front of a tank,
How bad would it have to be
To chain ourselves to the railings.
To rally,
To march,
To chant,
To protest.

To stand up for something, just imagine!
How much of the last century's pain
Are we prepared to squander
Before we even pen a strongly worded letter.

Imagine, if we cared as much for our principles as we do for our possessions,
As much for the environment we all share, as for the home we call 'mine'.
Imagine feeling the pain of someone, any one of the billions we haven't met,
As much as our neighbour,
As much as our partner
As much as our self.
Imagine the progress, when resources are shared.
And imagine if you can, the end game,
When we hear: 'Let's make America great again'
'We will Make Germany, *The Fatherland* great again',
'It's time to Make Britain Great again'.

So what should I tell them if they ask?
That we take more interest in the football?
That the living room needs decorating?
Or that at last,
...There's something decent on the telly.

Planet Tyson

Let's say, *It's a world away*.
The lesser of two evils,
Where (let's say) only dogs reside.
And where, after repeated upheavals,
The favoured persona,
The aspirational breed, is Pit Bull.
Ascending the food chain,
Descending hope's, fitful.

No other breeds control Planet Tyson.
All young, male Spaniels work to the template.
All young, male Collies chant the inscription.
Told that they must aspire to some strange mutation,
By teachers, parents: victims themselves,
The bullied, under achieved and disillusioned,
Abuse and indoctrinate
The same script, once beaten into them.

Labradors wearing thin smiles and uncomfortable new gear
Attempt the strut...
They get it soon enough.
Young, damaged parents impose the same narrative on their mewing pups,
While side-lined females,
With *obviously* less intelligence,
Stoop to roles of subservience,
To the dominant gender.
The deference they render,
Adopting the acceptable pose of submissive availability
To the most attractive of Pit Bulls in the immediate vicinity
That is, the wealthiest, most powerful of Pit Bulls, naturally,
Or face a lifetime of struggling, scarred from the lessons
And mockery.

What breaks the cycle
Of damaged parent to impressionable pup?
When media, commerce and politics
Are defiantly controlled by the most aggressive.
Supported by every breed under the sun,
Trying to disguise themselves
As snarling, muscular creatures   cont.

While circling and growling,
They fantasize tearing-off each other's skin
A weak, vulnerable creature to reveal
That they know damn well, resides within.
The same as they themselves conceal.

Planet Tyson.
Controlled by males
Adorned with every accessory that supports the image.
Driving their world
From behind their chosen symbols of success.
Motivated by greed,
Fed with vanity,
Controlled through fear,
And endorsed by the cowering pack.
No one dares swim against the tide,
Reciprocal pats on nervous backs.
The heaving weight of 7.7 billion likes.

And where's there to go
For the wannabe machismo dominator,
When the promises his parents made,
Fade, like the frivolous fantasies of some video creator.
He bought into Capitalists' blue nirvana: *dog eat dog*,
Fought for his life, only to find his lot;
An outcast in his own fantasy.
Dare he decry such a misplaced philosophy,
Concede, to not just failing to be the Pit Bull
That he never was,
But admit still
That his parents were naively feeding,
From the privileged hands of strategic breeding?
Or does he maintain the pretence,
With *Dear Deidre*, monosyllabic attempts,
To find someone, something, anything to blame.
Take it out on the blacks, the Jews, repellent of shame.
Them immigrants, the misses or the kids,
Passing on the baton that colours their lids,
Encrypting infant motherboard dressings
With evermore damaging default settings.

Pedigree Pit Bulls snore through the night
On full bellies. cont.

The others, howl at the moon between broken, tormented sleep.
Something's not right,
But they lost their instinct
When dignity was sold.
Snaffling scraps from the enlightened,
Living, just to grow old.
A world away (thankfully), on Planet Tyson.

Rob Kersley

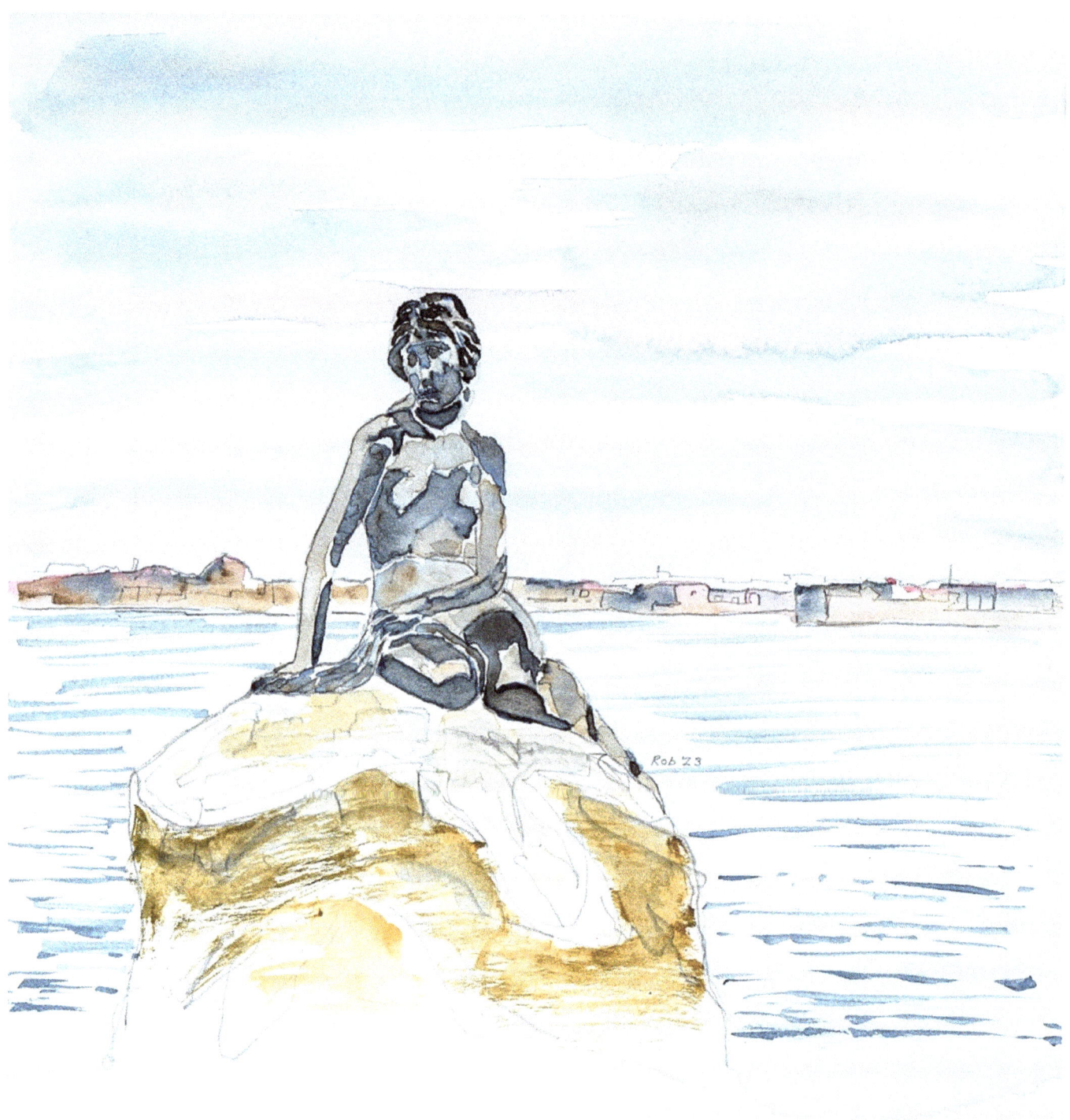

Between the Tides

Some towns appear to have existed forever,
Uncovered, by erosion from wind and whatever,
Great spires and spikes in extremeness of weather.
The wind removed sand that had lain there forever,
Hid avenues of trees and great parklands of heather,
Power plants and pylons that displayed our endeavour.

Copenhagen feels like its plug's been removed,
Drained now, to expose the deep channels it grooved,
Where canals remain full and its subways tattooed.
The deep, curving grids and copper roofs bruised,
To bright, mottled turquoise, defined and diffused.
Distressed oak framed houses, the Baltic infused,
Textured from submersion, at long last excused.

Sea levels push. They rise and they rise.
The conman in charge offers mere compromise,
As his truth within, is sacrificed for his prize.
With laughable tokens he dissatisfies.
Those scratch-card policies in transparent disguise,
The tide, always favourite to defeat his lame lies.
Mother ocean's love smothers, 'till she occupies.
In mourning blue veil,
Her tired earth cries.

Rob Kersley

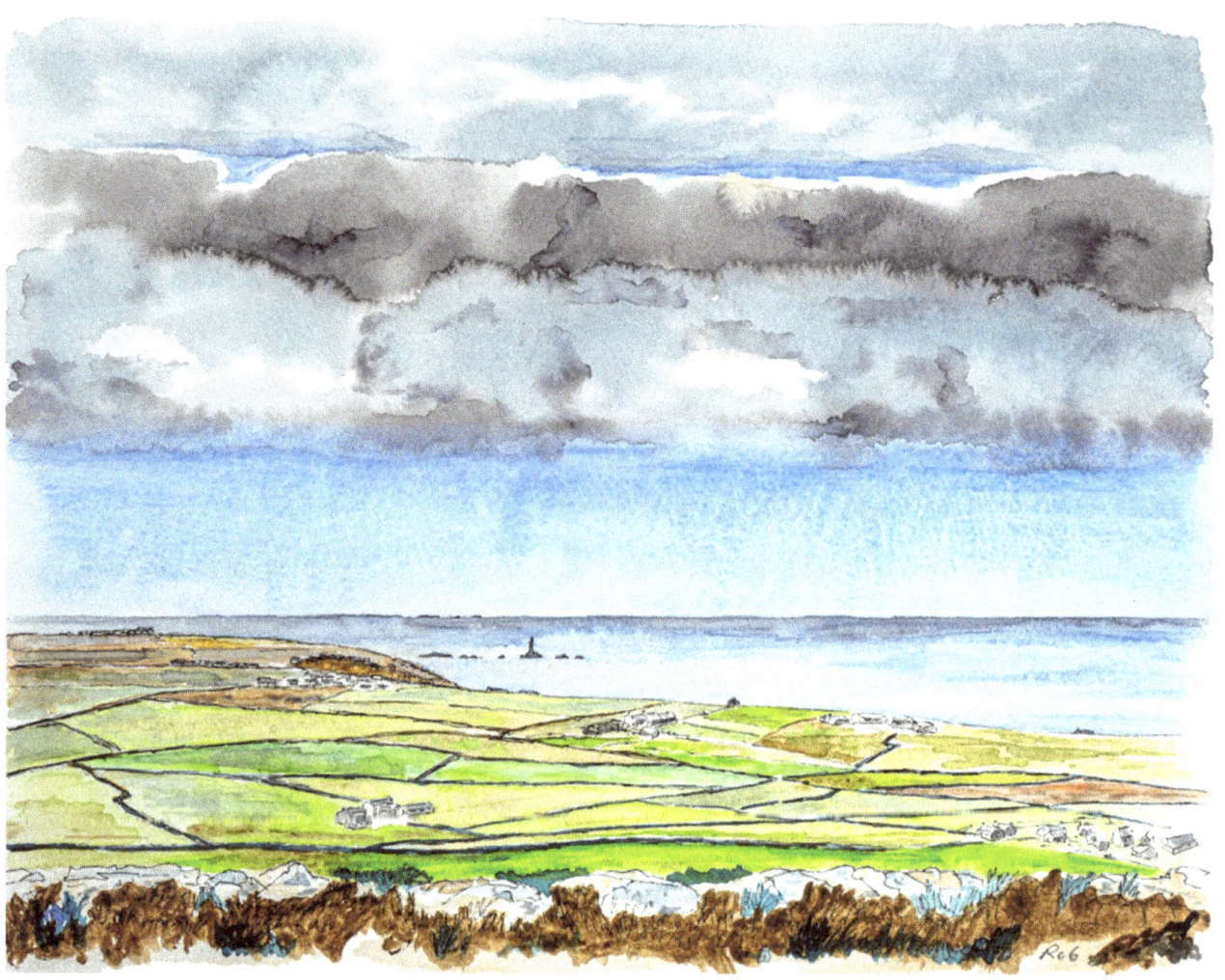

Au Revoir

Captivated, like a newborn in his mother's eyes.
Suspended in wonderment,
It made sense of the universe.
Billions of pin holes in an imperfect canvas
...And me.

It threatened,
Shook the ground for a trembling moment
With unexpected blasts.
An open window slammed. Shaken,
I cracked.

But when it's passed,
When it's just a memory stilled;
Those old eyes in a frame,
And the space they once filled.

With his ashes parcelled on my lap,
Barely keep it together
As I make my way back.
Sancreed, Tregeseal, Nancherrow,
His home.
It twists the gut,
Reaches way down and squeezes
Out the void he's left.
Mystified, in shock,
Bereft.
And everything's too bright,
Too loud,
Too numb to feel.
If only..
If only this final day
Wasn't real.

From North Rocks
He will look down on Gwynver,
And remember
When it was all so new,
Recalling days when he was too.
Noble head raised   cont.

As he breathed the spray.
Gazed into the milky flat pools,
Like newly opened oyster shells
That reflect the heavens.
Shallow and brief as life,
Terminal as the tides that carry them in,
Only to take them all away.

He squints;
Mothers, fathers, sons and daughters
Follows them out. Out to the ocean Atlantic
The life beyond the brief, bright waters.

As he sits and watches
And waits, he catches
Its fresh Northern Drift.
For now he understands this gift.
More learned then, than I could be.
He sits,
I pray
He waits for me.

Our Ken

I taped the games,
Just in case ...you know.
Played them all back
And watched as though,
Something once lost
Could be re-written.
But no re-matched fixtures,
No re-runs hidden.
The same results
But without the tension.
No edge of seat,
No apprehension.

But I play them every day of late
Usually after the news.
When I can't believe how blind, how deaf,
These Blue isles; confused and bruised.
For there lies a hidden antidote
For all that's so plainly wrong.
For when this sorry world steals my smile
And the road back feels too long.
When everything that gives me hope
Feels like it's held to ransom.
I sit quietly with a cup of tea
And watch Ken Owens sing the anthem.

They could sell it all around the world
Our biggest export ever.
Tros ryddid gollasant eu gwaed,
But our Ken would sing forever!
Special edition coloured vinyl,
MP3 downloads, CDs!
They'd be flying off the shelves all day,
Modern life would be a breeze.
Wales' identity restored once more
With customers given the choice,
Of a premium, luxury edited version
...Where they mute
Our dear Ken's voice!

Rob Kersley

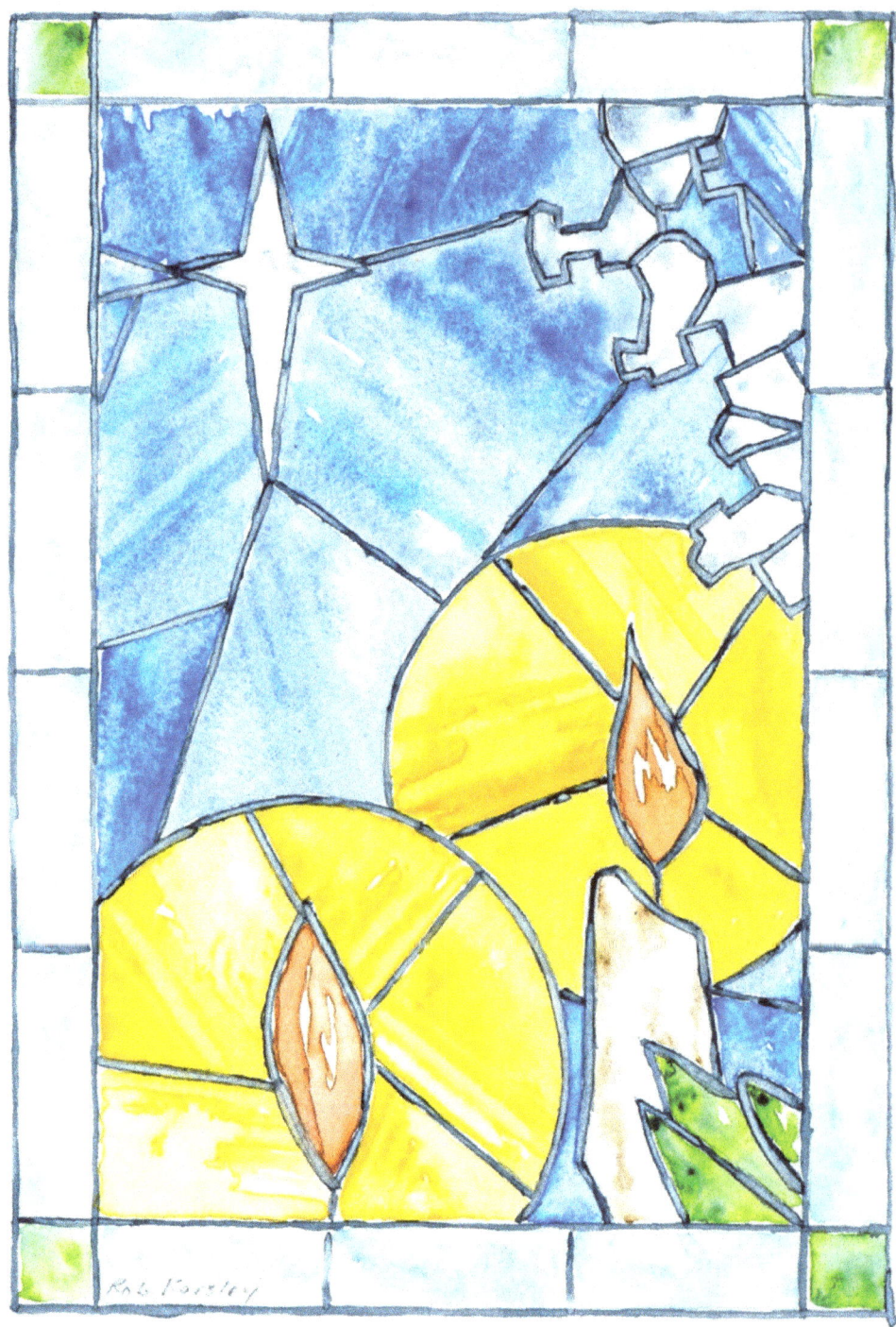

Together

Are you exhausted?
I'm exhausted.
I can't sleep for the storm
That's been raging outside my window.
Let me slip into the ocean,
Breathe the cool water,
Swim along the sand.
The ever quiet sea bed,
The tranquil calmness of the deep.
Fin along with my silvery friends,
Not wandering solo
As a lonely traveller,
But surrounded by others.
A shimmering shoal in an endless world of water.

Are you anxious?
I'm anxious.
Can't sleep for the turmoil
That's churning inside my head.
Oh, to fly;
To circle and observe the expanding horizon all around.
Leave land far below.
New pastures to be found,
With every beat of the wing,
Amid my familiar flock.
Not as some lonely, menacing hawk
But among my own kind.
Swirling, for the sake of swirling,
A show of unity
Dignity. Defying gravity.
Denying the wilderness,
Celebrating togetherness.

Another execution date comes and goes.
Another extension granted
And all they do with the precious time is squabble over the big chair.
Occasionally, they pull out a dog-eared,
Crumpled photo of the paradise
That they conned us into signing.
Their lies, Tip-Exed over.   cont.

It's a race to the bottom,
Shorting the Pound
To make The Sale Of The Century.
Like the NHS actually needs a pimp
In cowboy boots and shades
Under a comic ginger wig.

I looked back from Parliament Square;
A sea of faces.
A million of us,
With a million other things to do.
But like migrating salmon,
All of purpose
United in direction.
We swarmed through the corridors and rivulets to that place,
Flocked from all corners
Collectively to face
Down a threat
That preys upon division.
Because the wolf of the far right we thought dead
Has made his move,
Selling a drug to cure our dread.

He's out in the open, circling, fighting for survival.
Devious, clever and without conscience.
Knows if he can divide, he will conquer.
Knows we're exhausted and anxious
From this endless, endless,
Perfect storm of his.
But there is safety
And there is hope at least,
In unity.

Factory Settings

"If Brexit is a disaster, I will go and live abroad. I will go and live somewhere else."

Nigel Farage speaking on LBC Radio in 2017.

Source: The Independent

Rob Kersley

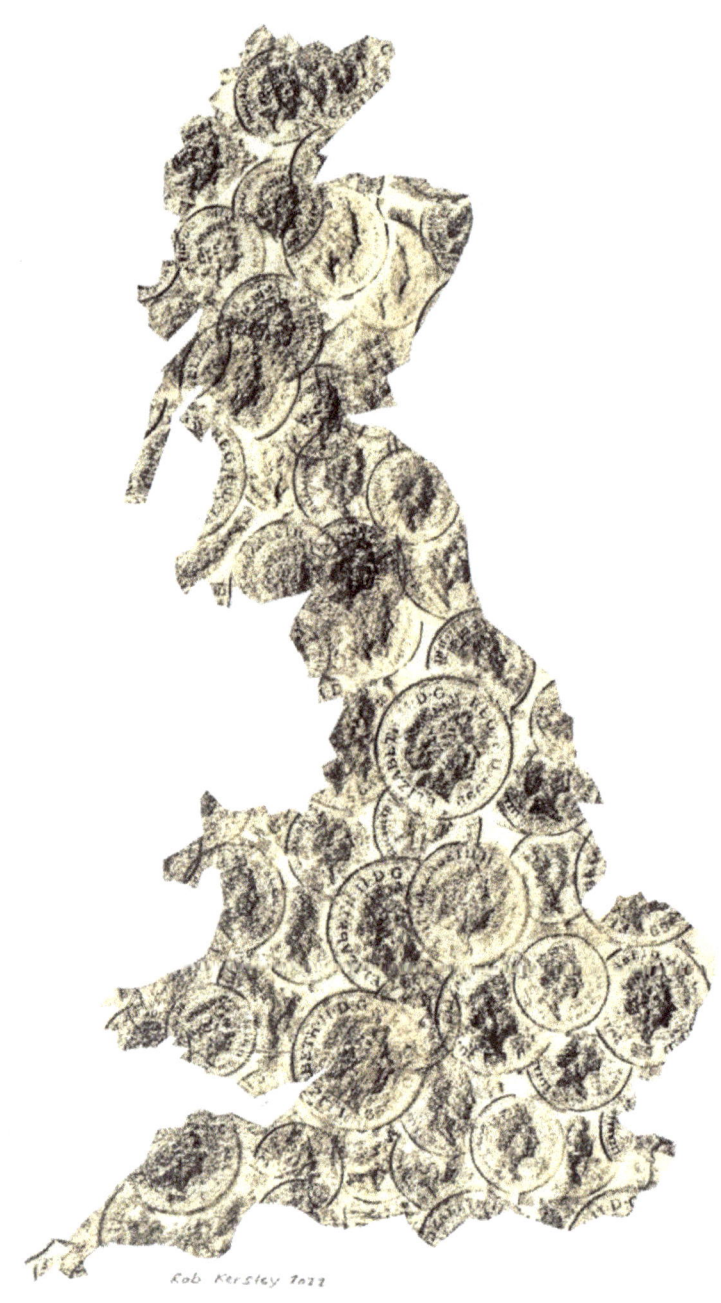

Windsor Barbie

A life-sized manikin,
With real nylon hair you can brush.
Electric blue eyes behind lids that rise and fall.
Bending joints,
And now, with gripping hands.

Pull the cord in her back
And hear her pre-recorded speech.
Pin the fur cape on her shoulders,
Balance her on her horse.
Stuff her into a plastic carriage
Then see how she waves.

Twist her crown down onto the synthetic head.
Perch her on her throne.
Paint a smile on her plastic lips,
Lock her up in rooms of gold.
Stick her rigid face on the front page
Then rip her family to shreds,
But bow down, fools!
Kneel before the tabloids' demigod.

The figurine in the palace;
Kidnapped, used and abused by the treacherous.
For men to lose their sight in her name,
Steel bayonets into the chests of innocent strangers.
Amputees sing hymns
With missing limbs.
Mothers will lose sons
Reduced to blood and pink mist
By horror that stuns
The wives made widows.
And ever- traumatized Privates. Shell-
shocked into a private hell,
Locked in a never ending battle.
For they can't tell,
When,
Why, or where.
...For what?
...For whom?   cont.

Not for them,
Certainly not for her.

What end could justify such means
When the more transparent the lies,
The more immune they become, it seems.
A monarch? ...rhetoric.
"Symbolic", of what?
Of an Empire for which we should beg forgiveness
Or of a public charade,
Of mock respect
By her own chancellors
Who lie and deceive.
Drag her by the lead
To "Sit!" and "Stay!". Maintain the status quo.
Or a symbol of victory in a class-war conceded by a public who've drowned their sorrows so many times, they can hardly stand to look at
A real woman,
To see her for what she really is.
Just a woman
Made into a doll.

A real mother.
Look now,
See how she cries
Real tears.

Minder

It's the only thing worth watching
The only thing, I find makes sense.
All I watch is repeats of Minder
I love what it represents.

I don't watch the news, or debates,
Or current affairs or any of that stuff.
And those sophisticated dramas,
They're just nowhere near enough.
I watch repeats of Minder on endless replay
All day,
Every single day.

Terry's great, a bit of a thug
But his heart's in the right place.
He beats people up, leaves 'em spitting teeth,
But not people like me.
All I ever watch is Minder,
And I cast myself as Terry's mate.

My favourite is Arthur Daley. I love Arthur, I do.
I know he's a liar and he rips people off.
And I know he's only thinking about lining his own pockets,
But he wouldn't rip me off, I'd be Arthur's friend.
I love that he gets a bit muddled, gets things wrong,
And yet I know it's all an act.
Deep down I'm aware, the creators know I crave imperfect innocence,
That that translates somehow as sincerity,
So they make sure that he's disorganized and forgets what he was saying.
'Cos that convinces me he's natural,
'Cos that's what I do sometimes ...right?

Thing is, when I was a kid, I'd get bullied by lads like Terry.
And Arthur, Terry's Gaffer, pulling the strings,
In sheepskin, sipping sherry.
Looking after his gang, doesn't care about the rest.
Slippery, sharp and shifty,
He's feathering his nest.
So I love Minder 'cos this time, I can be on the winning side.   cont.

I don't want anyone's love
And being looked after, I can't abide.
I actually don't want what I know is best for my family,
My town, my planet or my community or my country.

I just want the painful past to finally make some sense,
Forever seeking acceptance by the bully and the liar.
Childhood still shapes
The choices I make,
And that's why
I'll only ever watch Minder.

"In the end, we will remember not the words of our enemies, but the silence of our friends."

Dr Martin Luther King Jr, in his 1968 speech in Chicago.

Source: Forbes

Rob Kersley

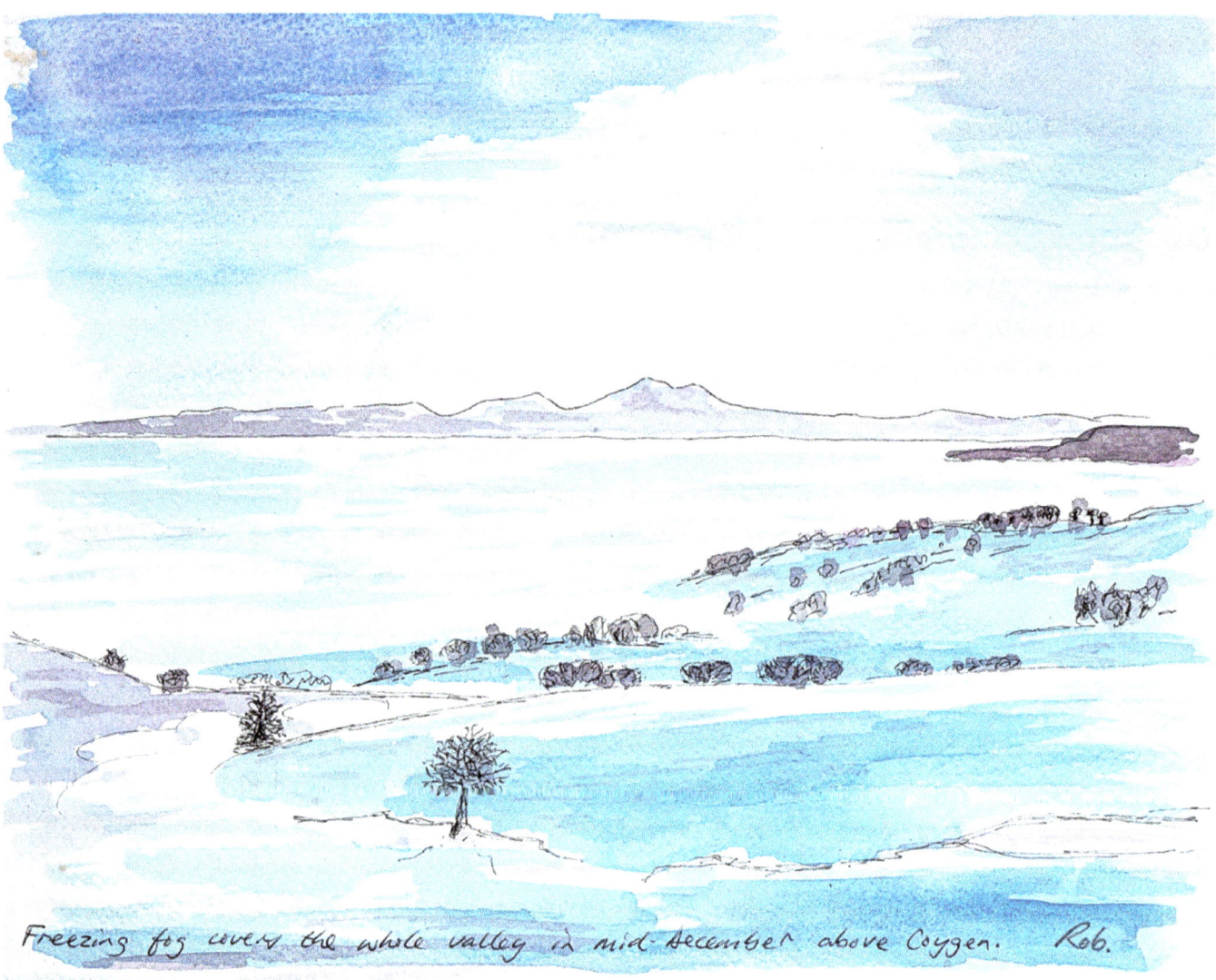

Freezing fog covers the whole valley in mid December above Coygen.   Rob.

A Clean Sheet

How many thousands of dizzying dashes of devotion,
For the humble, hesitant house sparrow.
Total sacrifice
For the flimsy, featherless flesh ...its child.

They strive
To flourish.
To survive
They nourish,
Against all odds.
In the face of relentless, merciless harshness,
Screaming gales around the eaves,
Icy rain on precarious,
Desperate beds of twisted twigs.

A brave robin,
Fiercely protective.
Starlings exuberant in mass celebration,
Murderous crows in canny communities
To an albatross
Or a dove;
Enchanted, endurance, enlightened,
In love.

For, if you're fortunate,
For, you did not earn
To be born to such a nest,
Then at some distant point learn
What your parents tolerated.
What they endured,
The burden they carried
Pale shelter secured.
Dried river beds of tears
Broke their banks years ago.
And they somehow...
They knew not to pass that painful baton.
Is this the greatest parental gift;
To allow their child
To start with an unblemished
Clean sheet?   cont.

A bitter sweet firebreak,
A parental stoic granite harbour wall.
Or a measured inoculation
Against the threat
They knew we too would face,
Like them
Like one
Like all.

Find your inner parent,
To shelter your hidden child.
Forgive yourself, yesterday's mistakes.
Stand naked alone,
What's done stays done,
Face down the storm and wash, atone.
Then move on.
Accept redemption in the deluge.
Leave the err
Of yesterday
Back there.
Forgive, look forward,
Always forward
Come what may.

What's this, just another day?
Did I awake to a false dawn,
This new page we've turned
Unblemished, not yet drawn.
Leave last year where it belongs
And focus, my friend on the challenges ahead,
There are so many.
Cry out to the heavens for peace
And it will find you.
Strive only for a happy life.
So give happiness today,
And be happy tomorrow.
Wipe clean your borrowed slate.
Happy New Year!
...This is, our unwritten
Clean sheet.

Swallows

South for the winter, warmer climbs.
Migration feels and follows
A jail break hatched within our minds.
As a pair of swooping swallows
Flying on instinct this one time
Taken aback by our good fortune,
Experiences to relish,
Opportunity to seize.
New memories
We hope to cherish.

Travelling as ever, light ...ish.
'Cos we're in the van of course
From the deck of the old Santander tub
I squint up, hearing dialects of morse,
Sweeping their perfect ultramarine wings
Two swallows up ahead
An iridescent cherry throat sings.
But we've got the laptop instead
And the sat nav. on the smart, smart phone.
While swallows avoid distraction
Do they sense the Plough?
I can't imagine how,
Magnetically, in the zone.

So we brought the last of the Christmas cake,
Some stollen and mince pies,
Like tiny birds grazing on the wing
With resolve behind their eyes.
We thought we'd bring the Scrabble
(We keep a running score),
But swallows struggle with the pieces
So they end up on the floor.
And the bikes of course
They're on the rack.
Some tools and tubes and lubes.
And shades and shorts and hats galore,
So we don't turn into prunes.
Jackets, coats and lightweight fleeces,
Shoes, socks and Birkenstocks.   cont.

Phone chargers and techy bits and pieces,
Squeezed into a Tupperware box.

Wetsuits are in
And the boards of course,
Ear plugs and wax and leashes.
Knitting ...(yes!), paints and writing pads,
Ice packs for my shoulder,
Tablets, glasses, boarding passes,
Some lip balm for my mouth,
Mugs and plates
And pots and pans,
Free as birds heading south.

Tickets, documents and passports,
Driving licenses, tennis rackets,
Maps and things to go on the headlights,
Breathalyser and hi-viz jackets.
Blue stuff for the chemical loo,
Scissors, nail clippers and dental floss,
Toothpaste, soap, conditioner, shampoo,
Tea bags, baked beans, soy sauce.
Fifteen books and last Sunday's paper.
We seriously considered taking the printer
Yes, as natural and free.
Travelling light, uncluttered, we
Are as swallows
Heading south for the winter!

Factory Settings

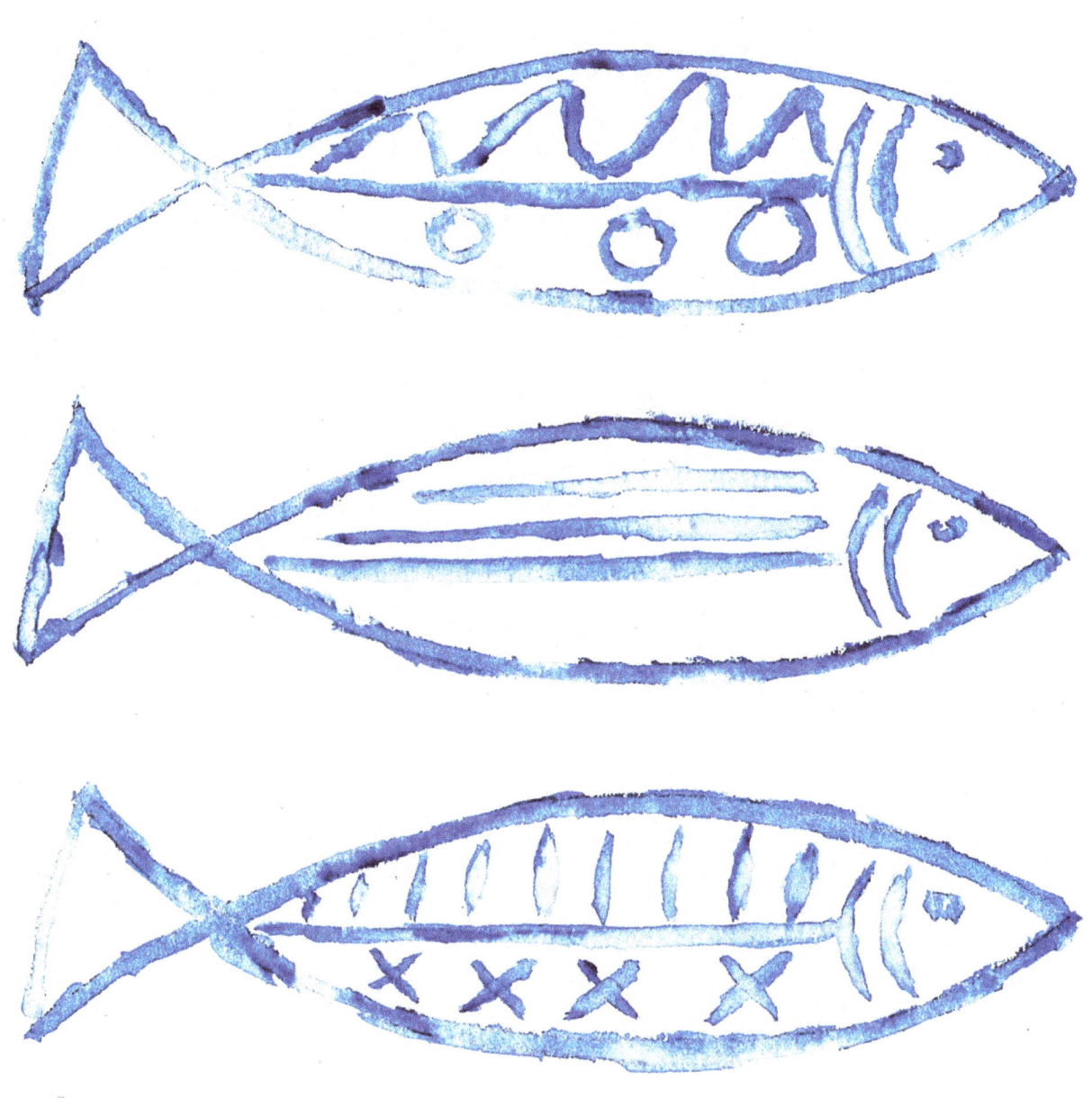

Dismount in Ferragudo

Roll into Ferragudo and step into a time lost,
A heavily embossed
Frame of mind.
A world away from the lip glossed
Winning smile of the superfast.
Where quiet beauty is tossed
Aside as landfill for another brownfield site.
Blurred lines crossed
When the price of culture is considered low cost.

Round the last corner, handlebars tremble,
Pencil tyres purr over the polished square cobbles.
I am an alien in lycra viewed by the leathery becapped locals,
Looking up from under shade, over draughts, through tobacco laced espresso.
Dismounting, on cleated, skating bike shoes. A warm chuckle
And open smiles as I hobble.

Remove my shades and feel the intensity of this, their sun.
The depth of colour and richness
Of their timeless world.
Squinting at the brilliant white elevations,
Under terracotta undulations.
Indian inked cormorants silhouetted on gunwales
In fixed fascination,
Of their fellow fishers, in observant occupation;
Net mending.
...Care, in communal concentration.

Blue windows, she smacks a rug in regulation
Time honoured tradition.
Bougainvillea lights up the gable in a scintillating, scarlet celebration.
And all I can think, through my ever more polarized lens,
Is how precious is this hidden place.
And how lucky, these unboastful folk
That we cut them loose,
Left them in twelve starred safe harbour,
As we concede to that inexorable pull
Of Americanization.

Factory Settings

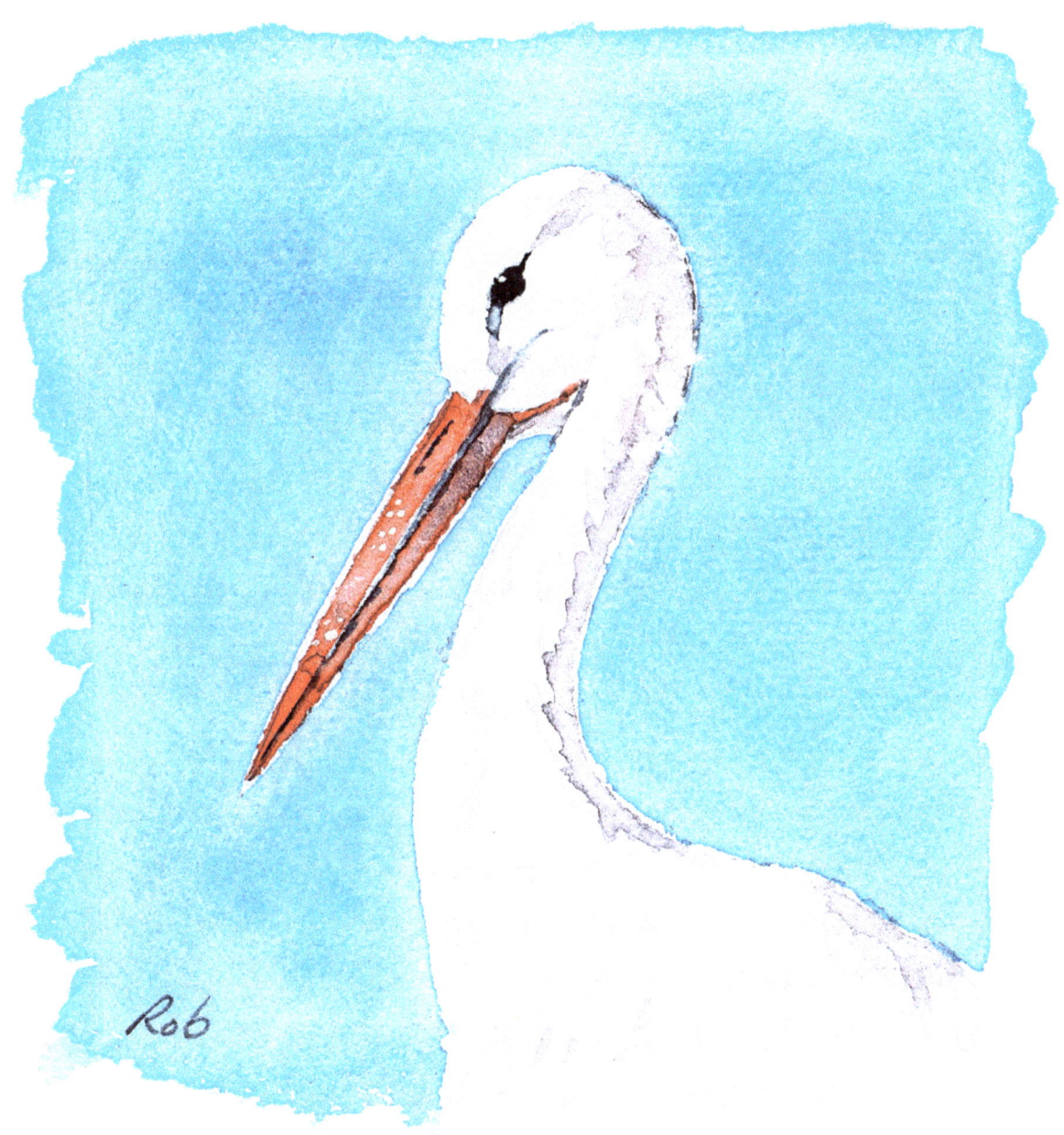

Beneath the Same Sky

Peering down at me
Sitting in pairs.
Or staring into each other's
Eyes, like tiny coals.
As sharp, stark, statues
In tangles of twisted twigs atop lampposts
And telegraph poles.
The oldest community in Estombar,
Part of the landscape.
Their vivid features, iconic as this cloudless sky
And the heat haze that pools on the tarmac below.

"What are they thinking?"
I was in a queue.
One aimed his silent, stare at me.
"You don't do much do you..."
I heard myself say aloud.
"...Lots of standing,
Plenty of sitting,
Seldom flying.
Fixed ...like glue."

Sometimes (but rarely) "hunting",
Which basically amounts
To standing, peering,
Occasionally picking, jabbing, stabbing
At the reeds.
"What a strange, non-existence..." I thought,
"While the rest of the world's in such a spin."
No stress,   cont.

No blackbird song
No tragic drama bleeds.
Everything safely measured
As polished knives and forks.
Just glide down from Northern Europe,
I knew all I needed to know
Of these drifting, distant Storks.

But he corrected me.
Put me straight as my squinting
Stare was met
Above the glinting
Windscreens.
He clapped his bill together,
Said, (by way of explanation) "We don't have a voice box.
We can't sing, but we say all we need
...And we dance."
He said, "...And we're not North European!
This is the Estombar family,
A large family
And this place is our home.
We fly for days
For the winter months.
In October, we meet in Sagres and take flight
Due south to Morocco
When we feel the time and place is right".

"...And no dramas, you say!
My neighbours, young couple, two years ago,
They were the only ones to not produce young.
They didn't understand.   cont.

How could they possibly know,

This, their only purpose, they tried and tried ...but no.

He became confused, so stressed,

Head was in a spin.

He went away.

Depressed,

He left

Her even more bereft.

She became sick. We watched as she moulted

She didn't eat for weeks

The certainty of our family

Jolted.

Then one day,

Humans came,

Took her away.

They just appeared at noon,

Came along that road

In this thing that rose up, high as the moon

On a limb

That stretched open,

Like an unfolding wing.

She said they put her in a cage.

She said they fed her through a tube like a reed.

That she drank a sweet water,

That she stayed still in the quiet,

Only waking to feed.

And it went dark for days,

But time went fast.

Said she thought she'd died,

That her time, must surely have passed."

                                                                                                cont.

"Then one day the men returned,
We could hear her.
She was hidden as it lifted her.
They opened the thing that she was in.
They settled her back in the same nest.
She looked around,
We circled above,
She looked so good,
So young
And full of life again."

"Soon after, her mate returned
Unexpected as the rains.
She took him back
Forgave her pains.
Her sickness gone,
They now have young.
But,
You knew all of that
Because, you knew all you needed to know."

"So what do you really know of me
Except this:
That I am here, sharing your space".
Every face:
A reflection of our own,
But playing the different cards they're dealt.
This place:
Where crickets' ratcheting
Chattering.
And laughter on the breeze,
A smattering.   cont.

Or a percussionist grating
Through topographic meadows
Of guiras,
That greet
Echoes through the olive groves,
Syllables muffled
Under this heat.

A curious building near the square:
Historic trading house
Preserved for some reason
In disrepair.
Elegant balconies, pretty roofline
Colourful graffiti etched on her skin
Stumbling, defiant
Like an African Queen.
In those last days that broke her,
The rich, earthy colours,
Warm shades of burnt ochre,
Exposed through her torn white washed cloak
In a sea of emerald,
Sprinkled with perfect white flowers.
The timeless tranquility
We felt sure
That we saw,
In the moments before
That fury of spinning dust
Tears down the valley.
Makes us hold our collective breath,
Chokes us for what seems like an age.
Stings our faces and blinds us.
Denied by King Midas,   cont.

A rampant virus
Torments and reminds us,
How alarmingly feeble our efforts
To reinvent and deep clean.
How desperate the responses
Of a world behind screens;
Socially distanced
In high definition
Dared dispel the very existence
Of the most powerful,
And the unseen.

Keeping our journeys to ourselves,
Watching others taking flight.
Humans and birds and every other living thing,
Every colour and every type.
Lost...
But for some pitiful words.

Heads in the clouds
That won't be denied.
But spirits so low
Can stay locked inside,
Yet... we come
And we'll go,
All beneath the same sky.

Rob Kersley

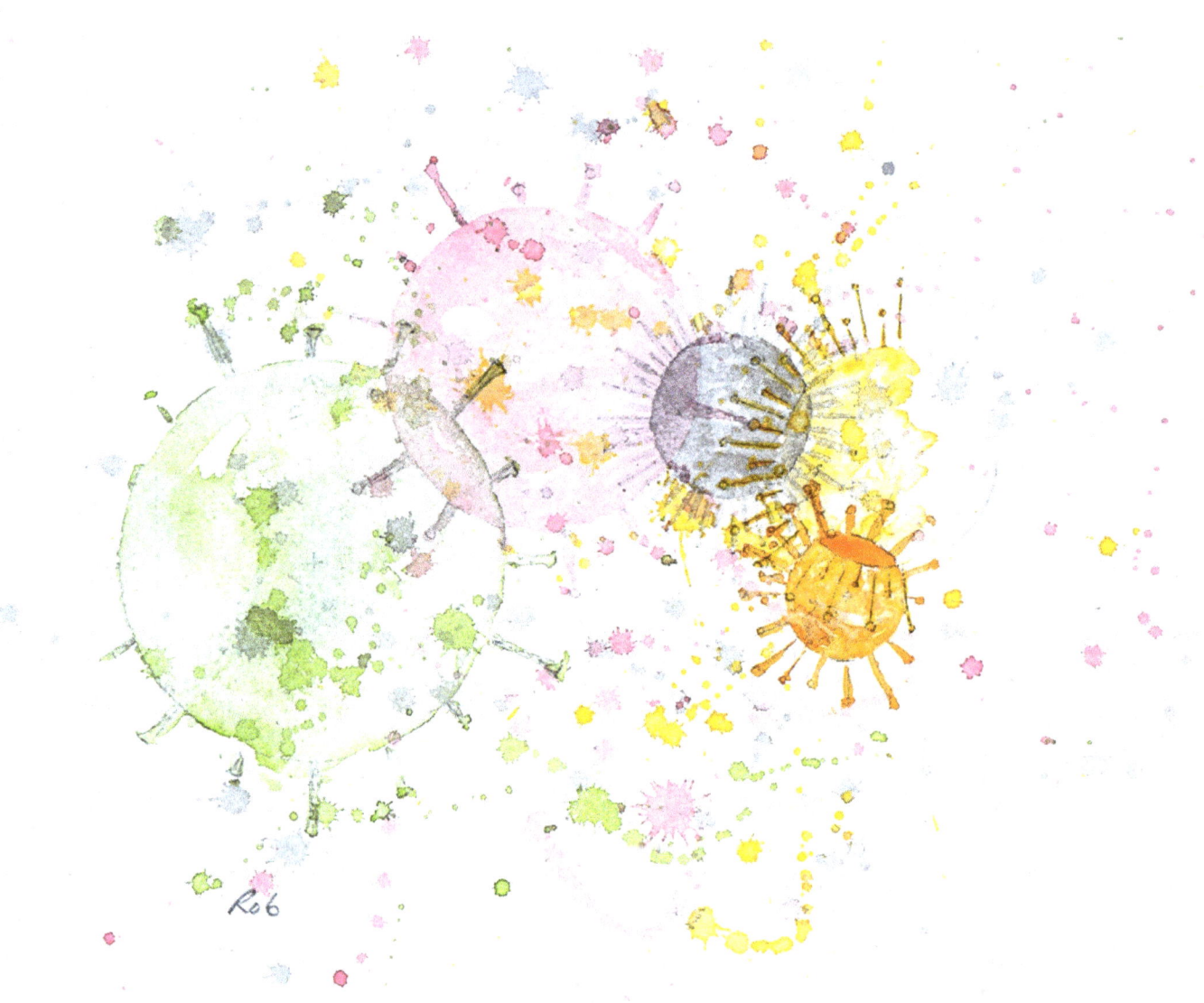

Stay Safe

Don't come too close.
Don't touch me,
Don't breathe,
Don't kiss,
Don't hold.

Stay away.
Stay inside,
Stay back.
Stay down,
Stay tuned.

Back in Newport,

The tattoo parlours
That specialize in Gothic horrors
And apocalyptic images
Have somehow lost appeal.
While kids in caps that were doing doughnuts
With oversized exhausts,
Fight instead, over hand gel
And toilet rolls.
The pressure building, shore to shore,
Reveals the character of nations
As never before.

We're locked down in Lagoa.
Not a child can be seen
Let alone heard.
Where short men and women
Stand in long queues.
Maintain a two metre air space
Silently shopping. .
Only two allowed in at a time,
No one's complaining.

Safe but stranded
Behind closed land borders.
Self isolation.
Portuguese pragmatism,   cont.

It seems, a contagion.
This microorganism
Of parochialism
With an ultra-realism,
Culturally distanced from wholesale opportunism.
Utilitarianism,
Left over ...postcommunism.

Nonetheless grim.
Fear paces its cell,
Within.
A maze
That replays
Like a castaway's days.
Inside.
Indoors.
Upstairs,
In beds,
Overslept,
Under quilts
Of uncertainty.

Don't contaminate,

Don't transmit.
Don't stop.
Don't start,
Don't give.

Stay home.
Stay closed.
Stay in place,
Stay put.
Stay the course.
Please
...Stay safe.

Factory Settings

"Boris Johnson agreed with some Tory MPs who thought Covid was, Nature's way of dealing with old people."

Sir Patrick Valance, former scientific advisor. Diary extract for Coronavirus public inquiry 2023.

Source: BBC News

Tips on Cutting Your Wife's Hair

Friends,

Whilst the suggestion of cutting your wife's hair because the hairdressers in Ferragudo are closed might seem like a good idea, the following offers some guidance for the avoidance of undesirable results.

1. Consent.
The signing of a consent form with text amounting to a disclaimer might seem excessive, however this is highly recommended. Casual comments such as, "I want a good inch or so taken off here and here", will be dismissed after the event even if you did take the trouble to voice record them, as will any caution you may have offered in warnings such as, "I've never ever cut a lady's hair before", or "are you absolutely sure about this?"

2. Mirrors.
Before commencing, remove all mirrors from the house. Their sudden disappearance might be difficult to explain but will almost certainly be better than the alternative.

3. Glasses.
If you normally wear glasses, wear them. Believe me, when I tell you that carrying on without them just because you had misplaced them; squinting or standing some distance away to get things a little more in focus is something you will certainly live to regret.

4. Consider Blood Sugar.
An excessively adverse reaction from your wife, might be lessened if nutrition levels are well balanced at the time of haircut completion. Extreme emotional behaviour at this highly charged moment might be explained by low blood sugar or dehydration, although it is advisable not to point this out by way of explanation whilst your wife is pulling her hair like she's trying to stretch it and making disturbing noises that you might not have heard before.

5. Fringe.
The importance of fringe aesthetics can't be overemphasized. Your wife will probably have her eyes closed to stop hair going into her eyes whilst you are cutting her fringe and may go quite rigid. She might even tremble slightly, this is normal. Be sure to keep her head level at all times as problems can be caused if her head is facing (even slightly) downwards, resulting in a much higher fringe than expected when she looks straight ahead. If this does happen stay calm and breathe normally. It is a mistake to try to correct it in any way, or to cut even more off the side bits around the temples to try to re-align the whole thing.

6. Acceptance.
You might be surprised by how much hair is on the kitchen floor when you have finished, as might your wife. It is best not to dwell too much on this sight, and whilst encouraging your wife to briefly view the clippings might demonstrate a degree of sensitivity, excessive examination whilst on her hands and knees can get a little morbid. Even worse, your wife might begin to pick some of the larger chunks off the floor and hold them up or even sellotape them back to reform her fringe and the side bits she remembers so well. Try to be firm but sensitive, as some degree of closure will be found

in the swift disposal of the removed hair. Please note that hair is not commonly recyclable in spite of what she might tell you. If you allow her to put it in with the plastic and tins, you might well find that she simply keeps fishing it all back out.

7. Counselling.
When you have finished work on your wife's new haircut and she begins to get used to your creation, some emotional support might be necessary. However, observations such as, "I've seen worse" or "It'll grow back", will not help. If cornered, say as little as possible, keep your hands in clear view at all times and try to look apologetic, pitiful but not hysterically positive. Also, whilst it might not be easy, try not to allow your eyes to keep wandering up to her new fringe or the side bits. She will pick up on this and it could further inflame the situation.

8. Spontaneous, Flattering Comments.
If you have the brain wave of asking a group of men working on the drains on the main road to Lagoa to make a spontaneously flattering remark when you both walk past later, make sure you communicate this clearly. If they happen to only speak Portuguese, use a phrase book or draw pictures on a sheet of paper. You might consider taking photographs of your wife's new hair cut (especially the fringe and the side bits and the top part) and show them to the workmen in advance so as to avoid the look on their faces when they tell her how nice her hair looks. If they begin laughing uncontrollably and pointing for some reason, keep a safe distance, these are particularly dangerous moments. Any bribe you might have agreed should only be paid upon a satisfactory outcome.

8. Just Say No.
Lockdown or no lockdown, it is strongly advised to resist any suggestion to cut your wife's hair. A hair band, an elastic thing or a hat is a much, much safer proposition!

Please take care.

Impossiblethornectomy

The fingertips that held the pens
That signed the notes
Unbound the ropes.
The fingertips that plucked the strings
That strummed
And stroked
That found the notes.
The fingertips that drew the face
That painted
Carved
And wrote for bards.
The fingertips that point them out
Divide
Anoint
Deftly disjoint
Them, single out.
This host was toast
Employ / exploit
In random posts
So quick, adroit.
The fingertips
That sowed the seeds
Their deeds
Succeed
Exact results.
The fingertips that pulled the pins
That laid the mines
That wasted lives.
The fingertips that fired the guns
And gripped the knives
That widowed wives.
The fingertips that swiped
And typed
That slammed the door
Then hitched
And hiked.
The fingertips that cooked and cleaned
In darkness help the blind to see.
Those fingertips that held me tight
That mopped this brow

cont.

That endless night.
Fingertips tucked me into bed.
Those fingertips kept
Me washed and fed.
Fingertips do
What fingertips are told
So soft of touch
But strong of hold.
Fingertips don't think
Yet they remember
Fingertips don't care
If we're here 'til November.
Messengers, servants
Obsequious instruments,
Accept commands
Share tender moments:
For first it grips its father's finger
And last, holds on to its partner's hand.
Innate precision
I can't do without.
But there's a splinter in mine
And I can't get it out.

Begging for an Encore

Is Malala taking a bow
Or bent double in exhaustion?
Didn't hear the standing ovation,
Then missed her lift.
So took the bus,
After another,
Endless
Double shift.

Malala's in her flat.
Sudden sweat,
Staring into the damp walls,
Edge of bed, shivering, sat.
The suited man still haunting;
One of the ones,
Who whipped up the taunting,
The tsunami of "Go home!" hate
And rode the tidal wave that rose,
As any would-be Head Of State
Of that unapologetically
Evil kind knows.

Half in a dream
Where she stands in a stadium, center stage.
Is that applause for essential key workers she hears now?
Or the crashing of a Mexican wave,
As ticker tape rains down.
Her shredded visa applications flutter all around.
Populist new immigration policy for a country once so certain.

She draws the depleted drapes,
Streetlights penetrate the gaps.
Rippling applause from our safe side of the curtain
As though begging for an encore.
With no idea
How we'll cope,
When Malala's sent away next year
From a land forever generous,
And lavish with soft soap.

cont.

So put your hands together for
Malala, Hasan and Neda.
Clap them, traumatized back stage,
The uncomplaining of this age,
The ones who toil for minimum wage.
Resounding, confounding,
These "Low Skilled" are indeed astounding.
Clap them all the way back to the airports,
And cross-channel ferries,
The millions to be let go.
While the man who ranted,
"Enough Is Enough!",
Lays very, very low.

Clap until hands bleed and heart aches,
Cheer for all you're worth
'Til every voice finally breaks,
Just like these,
Soon-to-be deportees.
The ones who still give so much for so little,
After travelling so very far.
Because the more that we say,
"We are not responsible",
The more, we must see that we are.

Rob Kersley

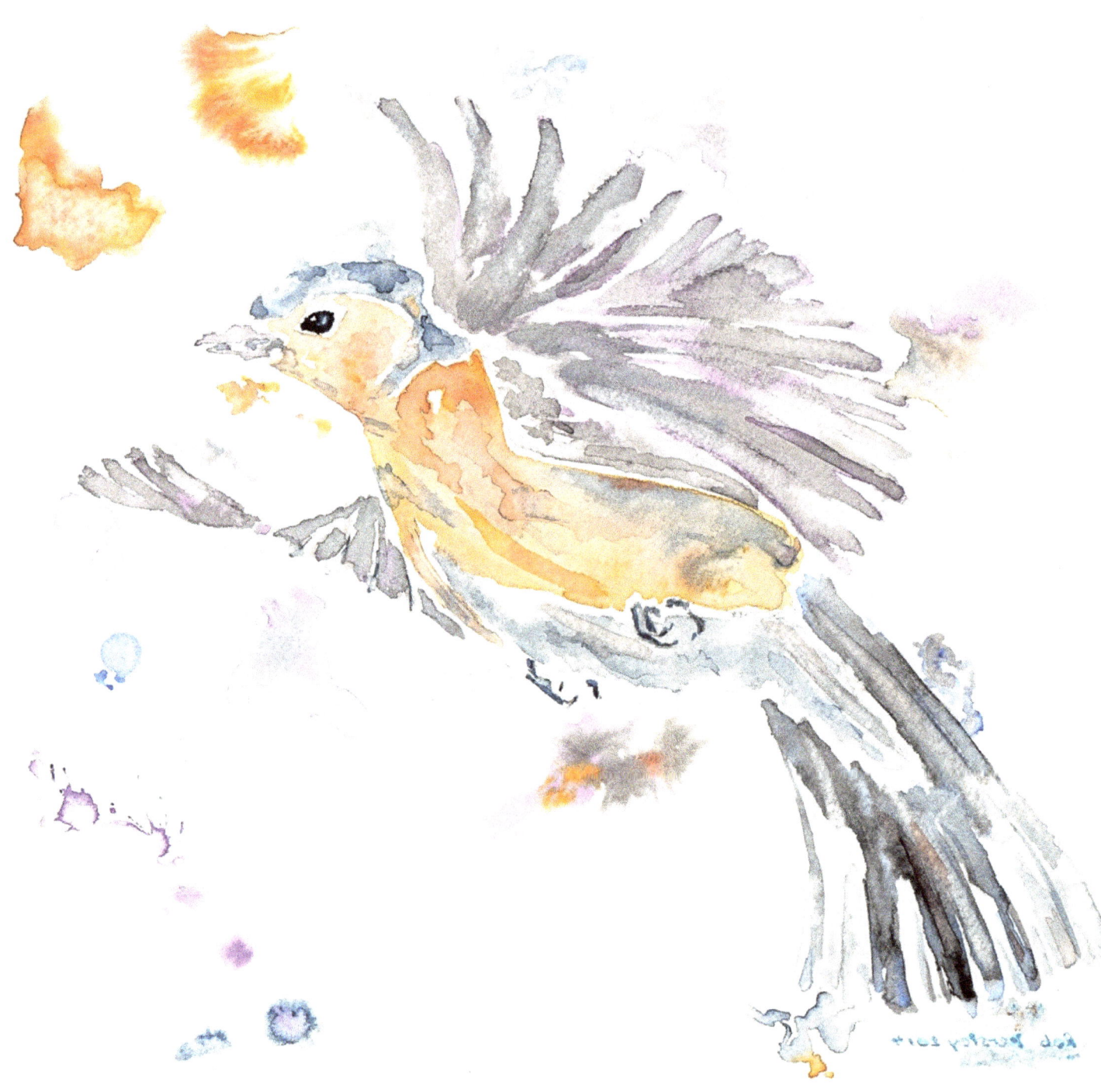

Bird Whisperer

Perhaps there was something
In that southerly Xaroco that would tame me;
Traces of cinnamon and columns of spiralling
Dusty sands from Marrakesh,
That seemed to slow her movement
As she quietly turned her head.
The moment before we could make some sense
Of everything that had gone before,
Of all that had been said.

The easterly that sprang up from Algiers
Blew wispy saffron strands across her face.
She patiently wrapped them around a finger,
Smiled,
And tucked them back in place.

Or was it the northerly
Veering down from Porto,
When lips that parted, softly closed again?
Words, sat back, inadequate,
When smiling eyes of sapphire, dropped
With emeralds and gold
Held in pale, glazed almonds,
Found in mine a home.
Captive, in the softest gaze
I could not help but hold.

I remember the steaming westerly
Carried across from the Azores.
And all we thought we knew back then
But no clue what was held in store.
With wings tucked tight in her careful hands,
She could fling me high to the great, blue wide,
And no matter how those winds pulled me now
I would circle back down,
To her waiting side.

When We Go Back

Back home...
They say that from gardens
That were never so neat,
People chat across
The trafficless street.
Checking on neighbours
From the edge of their pavers,
Putting health and social behaviours before all.
Someone must have hit Reset,
Messed about with the lift.
Sent us all crashing to the lowest floor,
The entry level
Of Maslow's law.

Us? ...Yeah, we're okay thanks,
Worse places to be stuck ...that's true!
But it's strange to find
We spend a good deal of time
Reflecting
On the how
And the why
And the what, that we do.
It is lovely here,
The colour and the pace,
Interacting in such a different race,
Where the sun shines on this
Analogue face.
We're safe
But we're clearly not of this foreign land.
So yes,
We need to get back when we safely can.

We all need to get back,
Return to some, Normal.
But when we're finally back on board,
Once we, "Fire up the engines of the economy.."
Will we still publicly applaud
The Essential
...The absolutely essential Key Workers:
The Carers, the Drivers, the Porters and Cleaners?   cont.

Once we Fire up those engines,
Will we be running so hard to keep up (for example),
That in the stampede,
Fail to see
What we trample?
Once these Engines are fired
And they gather momentum,
Will we challenge our goals
Or dare ask the question?
Did we trade our best years
To buy stuff we didn't need,
Obsolescence assured,
Discontent guaranteed?
Will we, superhumans
Willingly supersede
Early morning bright birdsong
When we're up to full speed?
Will we still notice the dew drops
On a fragile, young petal,
As we thunder along
Demonstrating our metal?
'Cos whole weeks can flash by
As the tempo gets faster,
When we march to the band
Of an imaginary master.
Eyes locked on, and hands free,
Will we use our potential
To connect
With our planet,
Appreciate
The Essential?

So...
When we go back,
Which, we eventually must,
Can we take just some
Of these
Essential things with us?

Rob Kersley

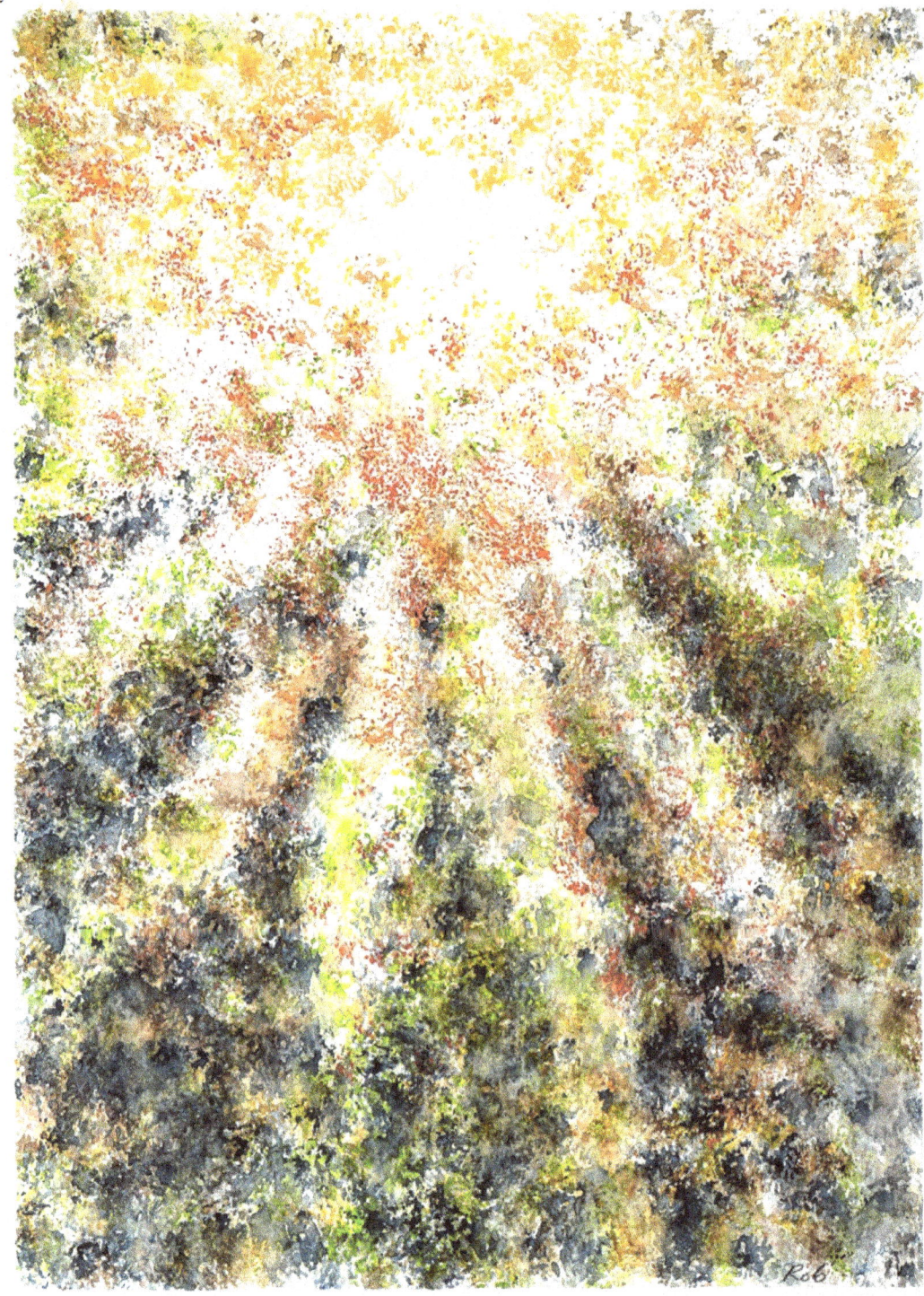

Don't Stare Into the Sun

Don't stare into the sun,
Nor claw at the ground,
Searching for answers,
Not ready to be found.

The burning
Eternity,
Of an absolute
Agony,
Will leave us
Asking why.
But light and life
And warmth and love,
With time
Will pacify.

Closed eyes, in solemn acceptance,
Of where all beginnings begun.
Your search could leave you blind
My love.
...Don't stare into the sun.

Hush Little Baby

Hush, little baby, don't say a word,
Papa's gonna give you some guidance blurred.

And if that guidance blurred don't work,
Papa's gonna give you his adorable smirk.

And if that adorable smirk seems cool,
Papa's gonna send you all back to school.

And if that school, so crowded throbs,
Papa gets your parents back to their jobs.

But your job is to Stay Alert,
'Cos Papa's no idea where the virus lurks.

And if that virus is carried back home,
Papa will encourage your folks to roam.

And if they roam, and the virus transferred,
Papa will have immunized the herd.

And if, for that herd, the death knells ring,
Papa will just tell you... "Hindsight is a wonderful thing".

No Harp, No Wings

I thought I saw an angel
But I couldn't see her wings.
Though she filled the air like an symphony
That danced along the strings.

She must have left her harp somewhere,
For it wasn't in her arms,
Which were guiding her young children.
As they clasped each others palms.

Was that another, near the bus stop?
Beneath her hood, I watched her face.
The cold rain lashing all around her,
As she tied her daughter's lace.

Then a male one at the school gates,
Kneeling, to look her in the eye.
Zipped her coat and wiped her tear,
I didn't get to see him fly.

I'm so blessed I know, that I still have mine
I FaceTime now, in these strange times.
They're on my phone ...and then they're gone,
These days screens connect our lives.

A love divine must be the giving,
A whole life of simple things.
'Cos last night, I saw both my angels,
I didn't need to see their wings.

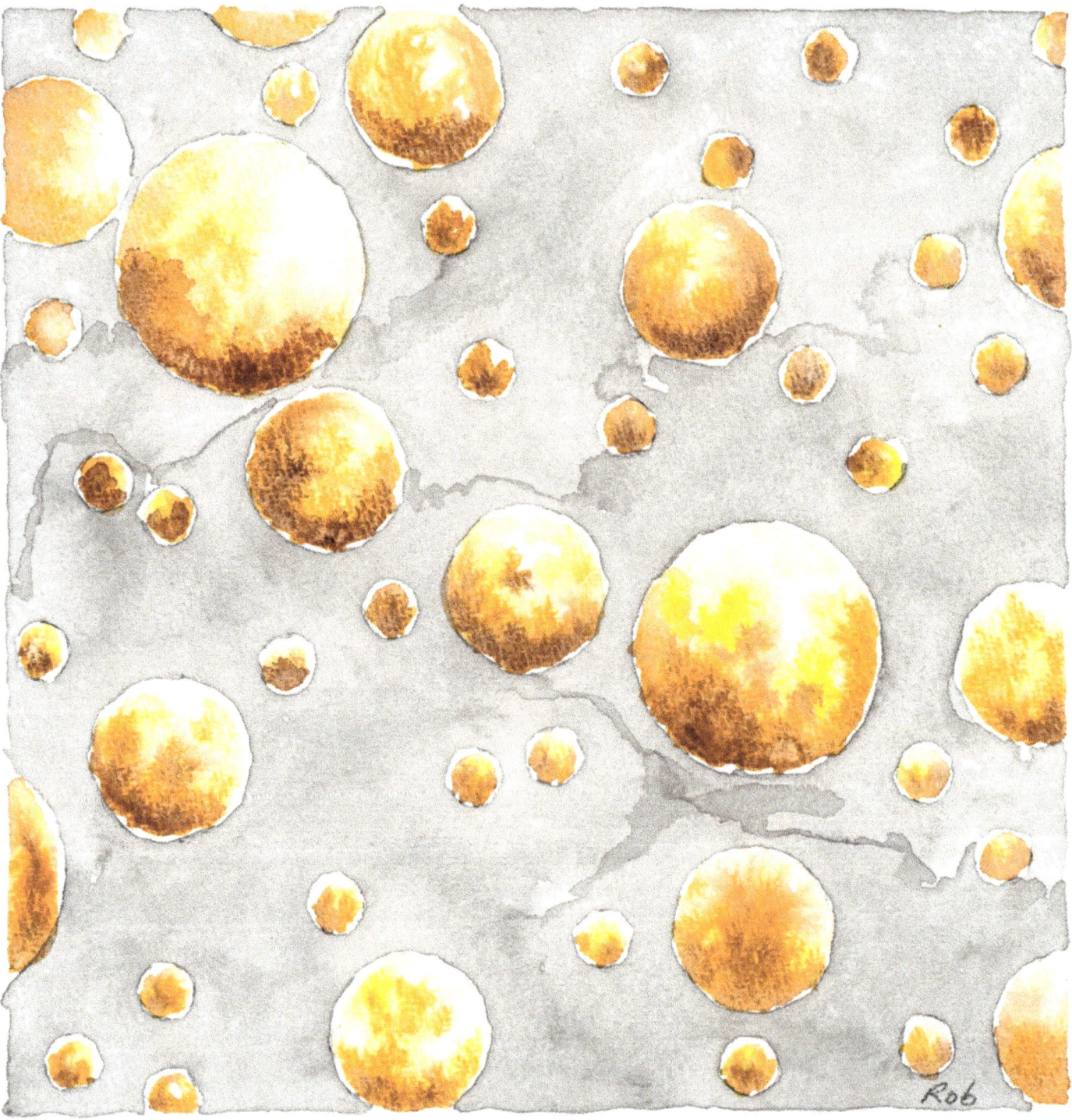

No Price Tag

I sensed that something fairly heavy was coming my way,
And so it passed.
It took him a while
But he settled at last.
He had fidgeted and fiddled with the folded napkins
Long after the others had turned in
So that now, it was just me and him
Sat around the debris of that dinner table.
He talked around the subject, circling nervously.
I studied his abstract origami creation
He had set
Between the table mats and the condiments,
Amid the crumbs of the evening,
Then looked up at his familiar features.
When at last, he took a long breath and raised
His shadowed face to meet my gaze,
He explained his difficult dilemma,
How he had arrived at this now seemingly inevitable junction.
I listened and sipped water from a wine glass
Before offering up an observation:

"You're asking,
What will your love earn?
Will your considerable outlay
Have a guaranteed return?
Could this indeed be paradise
And would such a life be worth the price?
We're talking of a whole lifetime of love here.
Weighing up the cost of your devotion. We're
Debating if your plan is rational,
As though this undertaking,
Could be measured,
Conventional,
Or practical,
Transactional."

"There's no price tag and no brochure,
As in a gallery of pure allure,
Valued only in subjectivity,   cont.

Where sensitivity
Assumes
That commitment will only ever be groomed
For the all-consumed.
Where the ultimate creator
Seeks to find a perfect suitor.
The price may mean everything to you,
Or perhaps nothing at all,
For what you see before.
Such a blindfold decision
To ensure the provision.
Disregard your superstition
And embrace the brave collision,
Because, this thing...
You just don't know what it will bring."

"But you did know:
At first sight
That warm smile was so bright.
Lively words did alight,
And her laughter took flight.
Took your breath as you might
Find someone or a part of
You that
You traced,
You'd forgotten,
You'd misplaced.
Spoke to you in crystal tones, interlaced
With a freshness and cleanness. Her newness so chaste,
Yet oddly familiar.
Then caressed, 'til the night
Met the sun streaming through forgotten windows to ignite
Celestial shafts of pure white light,
To expose and indict
Those dusty corners of your world,
Found the truth on your flags
That would at last, be unfurled."

"I do understand,
It's like you want to unmask
These emotions, these feelings,
A generation stretched out and a future to bask
In the glow of her love,   cont.

Do you hear what you ask?
What will her endless passion and devotion take from you?
But love is blind,
So close those hungry eyes
Then see what you find.
If this absolute beauty compels you, commit
All that would otherwise be hoarded.
Because if you have to ask the price
...Then I'm sorry, you can't afford it."

I still remember that night,
Sat alone in the half-light.
Staring into the mirror,
That overlooked the dinner
Table, emptied of food,
And just myself in reflection,
Reflecting the mood
As I patiently waited
For me to conclude.

What a moment that was,
One I'll never forget
A journey led by the heart,
That I never
Would regret.

Rob Kersley

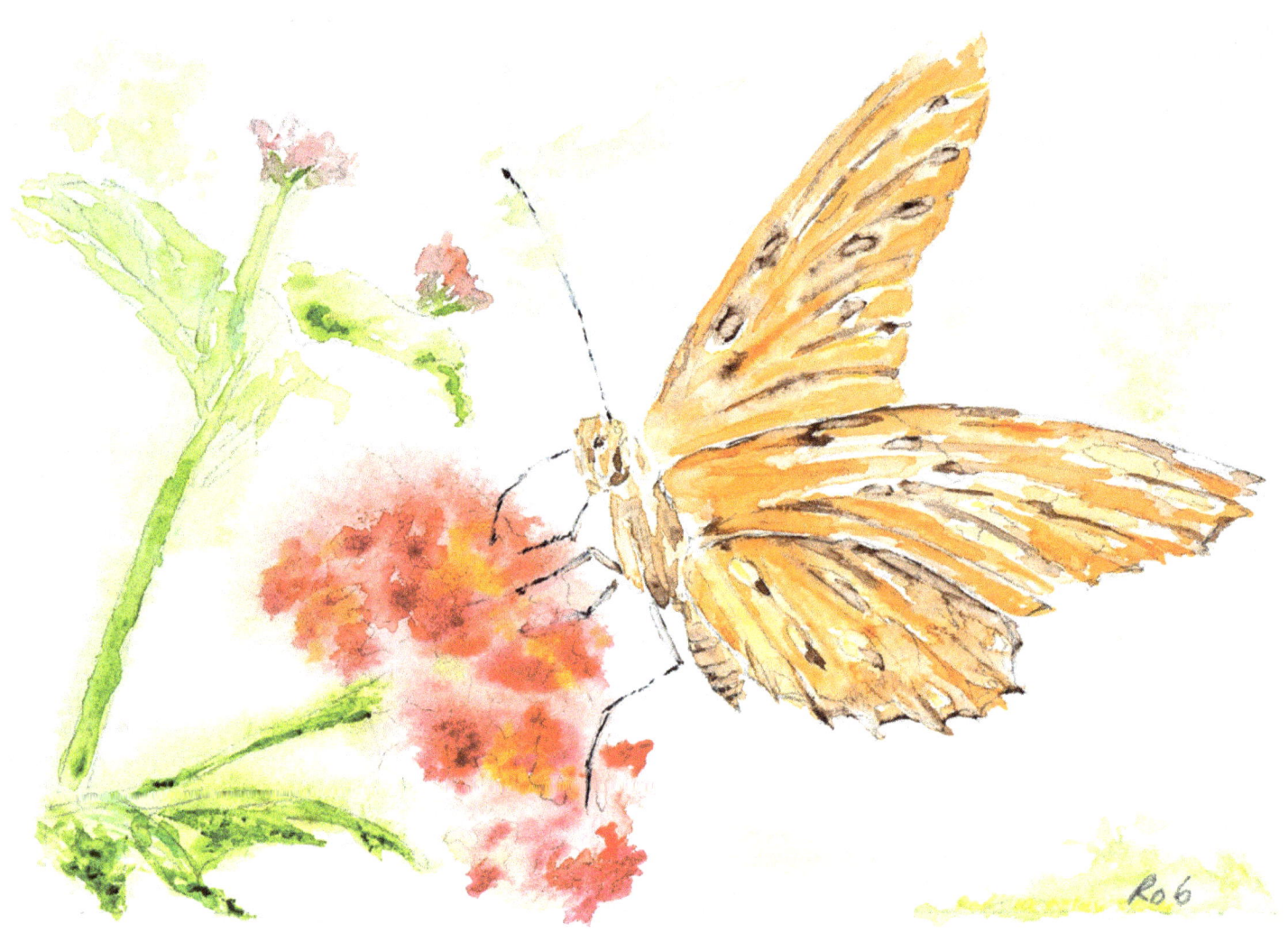

Pain of Life

I've heard it more than once,
That ancient wail
Of a soul emerging,
Of a birth.
The searing pain of new life forcing its way into the world.
The very first pain, felt through every sensory nerve ending,
And suddenly, simultaneously illuminating
Swathes of microscopic receptors.
Igniting a new brain,
A new mind,
A new life.
And then almost as suddenly,
It subsides.
And the quiet. The peace, the tacit relief.
The strange calm that descends like a blanket.

I've heard it more than once,
Those desperate gulping cries
As one slips away,
Of a death.
The agony of elevation, the enforced detachment from this world.
The fateful, finality forsaken.
The last, glorious leaf
Of a book, closing its pages to sleep
But not to awaken.
And then almost as suddenly,
It subsides.
And the quiet. The peace, the tacit relief.
The strange calm that descends like a blanket.

Someone died yesterday in Brazil.
In New York,
In Madrid,
Many died and many born
Into and out of this strangely strained arena.
Why do I fear it so?
Why, when my head tells me something,
When I think I understand that life has to make room for growth.
That death is an inevitable mystery
And life, an incomprehensible miracle.

cont.

Why then, must my heart break in spite of what it thinks it knows?
What it hopes it knows,
What it knows it breathes,
What it believes it knows,
What it knows it believes.

I rode out through Portimao
And let rip some energy,
Up to a mountaintop town called Alferce,
Trying to leave this difficulty back there in the traffic.
Pandemic death rates throbbing somewhere inside since I read,
Now, trying to leave it in the turmoil,
In the stifling heat of the city with its patient, masked, frightened, poor people.

Past the cemetery,
Past the hospital.
Beyond the care home and the nursery,
I left the city limits and climbed high, on a twisting, snaking
Ribbon of silvery tarmac,
Early shadows yawning and stretching
In front of a red, rising sun.
I climbed alone through forests I'd seen devastated
By fire when I first arrived;
The miles of cork and eucalyptus, blackened from last summer's inferno along these mountains.
I looked and saw what I expected to see;
Black, charred bark, no colour, no life
And nothing in between, no grass, just scorched baked sienna soil,
Cracked, hard, stony ground.
Until I looked again.
The green of new life was pushing through
...Unbelievable!
On the tips of the branches
Bright leaves unwrapping themselves slowly, one by one.
Delicate but determined,
Forcing themselves,
Squeezing themselves out of the derelict husk.
Into the light,
From within ghosts of trees, distorted and twisted,
Contorted, resisted as the fire must have whipped the furnace of wind around them,
Reducing their flesh to incinerated carbon.
And yet all the while,
Deep inside,
Perfected, contained.   cont.

Protected, remained
This seed of life.

I came to stop
At the top.
Transfixed by one, standing on its own, overlooking the devastation. Black
And burned with its statuesque trunk arching back,
So that its face looked up to the deep, endless sky
And its charred branches and brittle finger tips reached up to the heavens.
Animated, in the most powerful way.

She

(Charles Aznavour, please forgive me for this!)

She, may be the face I can't forget,
Confounds my state of mind and yet,
May be my treasure, or the price I have to pay.
She, may be the song that summer sings,
The sweetest chords or pulls my strings.
Can want a million different things
Within the measure of a day.

She, may be the beauty or the beast,
Attempts mad things with flour and yeast,
That turn each day into a heaven or a hell.
She, can make the dinner of my dreams,
Her smile maintained despite the steam.
Meringues she beats to the extreme,
Omelettes, as well.

She, who always seems so happy in a crowd,
Who speaks her truth with her head unbowed.
The hounds of falsehood dare not look her in the eye.
She, may be the love that cannot hope to last.
Digs all sorts of stuff up from the distant past,
So I'll regret them 'til the day I die!

She, may be the reason I survive
And though at times I duck and dive,
Sometimes it's scary, when she's going through the gears.
Me, I'll take her laughter and her tears
And make them all my souvenirs,
For where she goes, I've got to be.
The meaning of my life is she.

The Brits are Coming!

White, slatted shutters on bedroom windows remain closed.
Carvoeiro is getting used to sleeping in.
A cafe owner paces (caged), his stretch of cobbled road.
Polishes glasses, kills some time, adjusts napkins.
From fables of remaining touches
Tables will, untouched remain.
To glance his watch,
And stroke his tie,
And then check his phone again.

Sun loungers and parasols arranged along a perfect beach,
Immaculate, gleaming grids of white and blue.
A temperate, attendant,
Will proceed to dust each one,
To clean the slate and purify the view.
The obsessed eradication
Of any whiff of stale, stagnation,
Justifies his fragile station,
More in hope than expectation,
That if he's looking busy
It maintains his reputation.

Faro, for now,
Has been stood down;
Skeleton staff arrive, just kids.
A manageress updates her screen.
Overseas her failing crop
Observes the worst
From under heavy lids.
Accommodation is all but sacked,
She twirls her bobbled hair
Like the twitching tail
Of an irritated cat.

And hire cars, trapped by trammels,
Line blank freeways in vast channels.
Estuaries of glinting panels
That stretch for miles and miles and miles.
And over those horizons,
Undulate seas of rising tensions.   cont.

Fifty thousand cars redundant
Parked-up, passive, lines,
Despondent.

But fear not,
The Brits are coming!
...Just need to find a flight.
The Brits are coming soon enough
To make it all alright.
The Brits are coming, yes they are,
They've re-scheduled travel plans.
The Brits will come, stand by your beds,
In Lynx and fake Ray Bans.

Cutting the tags off new Havaianas.
Packing shorts in lurid prints
Of purple palms and green bananas,
On some River Island chintz.
Having ransacked George at Asda,
And old Matalan as well,
Yes, those Brits are coming mighty soon,
In search of San Miguel.

Oh yes! The Brits at last are on their way,
And they're chanting football songs.
A re-kindled spirit of '66,
They're dropping Jager Bombs.
A Carling goggled aging empire
Strides Portillo-like, erect.
Then accessorized with a soaraway Sun
And dressed by Sports Direct.

The waitress will smile politely,
Taking orders from the rude,
Given of course in the only worthy tongue,
Clears the plates of picked o'er food.
Sweeps the streets of broken bottles,
And chip cartons, from the floor.
And a beer soaked Super Dry t-shirt
Wasted.
As the night before.

cont.

Soon the Brits will swarm like locusts,
Roost high rise to bed thee down.
There'll be bread on the locals' tables
If some vomit on their town.
Beach bodies swell a hundred fold,
As economies dictate.
Yes, the Brits are coming soon enough
...I bet the Portuguese can't wait.

Rob Kersley

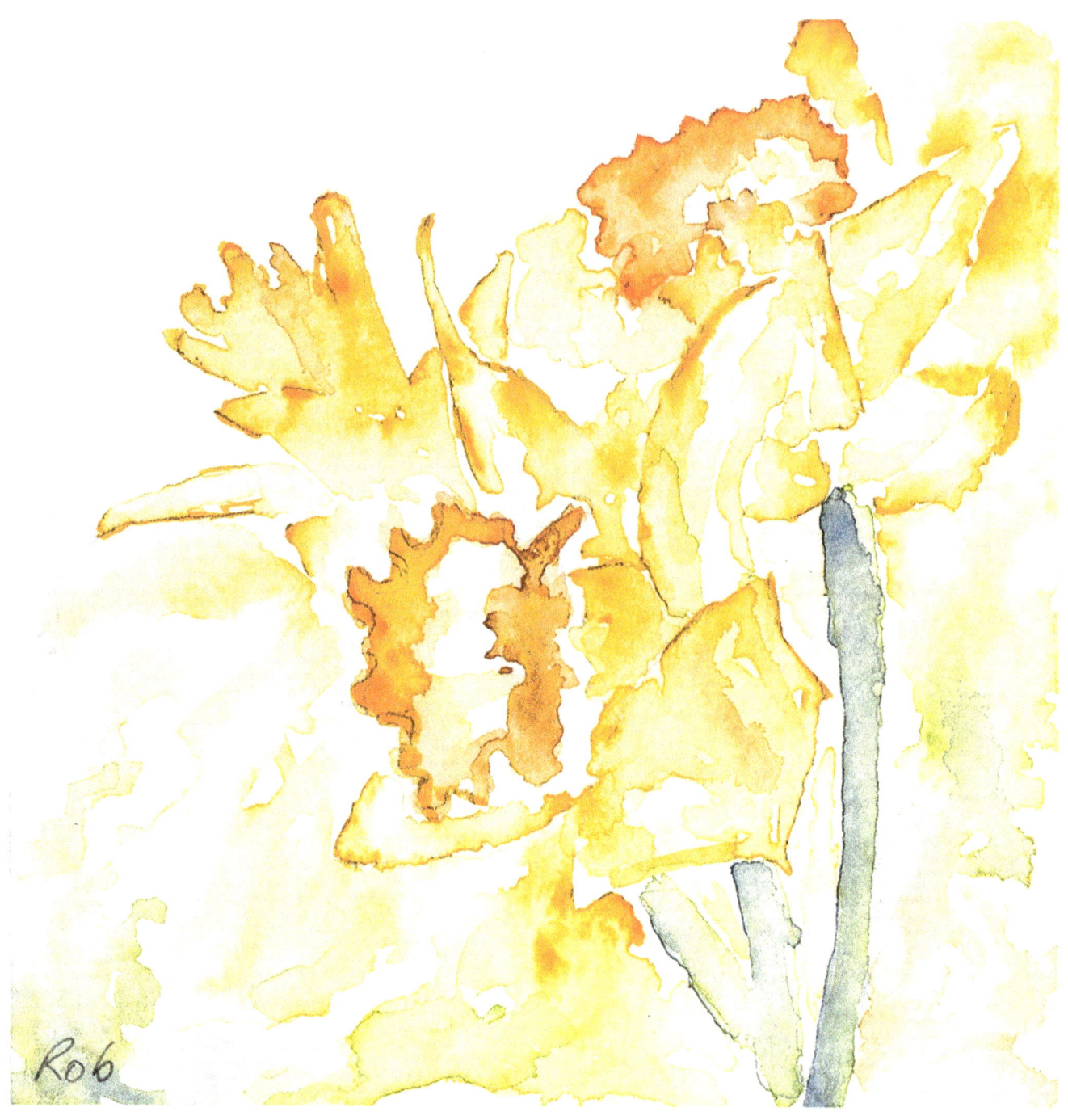

Acknowledge

There's a fly on my window, trying to get out.
 A four thousand lens eye, but blind
  Like a drought
   Of the vision to begin
    To navigate from within,
     To find his way out
      The same way he came in.
Despite all he can't see
 He believes he retains
  All information at hand,
   Yet devoid of the ways
    To save himself from himself,
     Trapped inside the bright glaze.
Though he's totally lost now,
 His searching grows shorter!
  Throws his babies away
   With their tepid bathwater.
    Disillusioned by the doctrines
     In whose names he saw slaughter,
      Rejects everything spiritual
       To enact a new order.
But the space that was joy
 Is so swiftly debased.
  On his face, just a trace
   Like some poor soul displaced.
    Whole communities unlaced,
     His grace sadly residual.
      A new religion to acknowledge;
       He ordains
The Myth of the Individual.

Accept

I was lost,
In the dead of night amidst the strangest of mazes
Of narrow, cobbled, gas lit streets
Within Dickens' Victorian monochrome pages.
Then set the hefty book down for a moment,
To consider, such days of poverty in those damp, diseased dark ages
And the perpetual
Seed changes,
In our comfort and liberations,
Compared
To their not so great expectations.
Then attempted,
To extend that same trend
Through intervening machinations,
Forward,
To future generations.

The corrections needed,
The work as yet unseen
To redress a toxic legacy,
For our great grandchildren in between,
Who will have no time left
And no choice but to intervene
In the old misplaced trajectory.
Reconfigure the machine.
The ones who will have to acknowledge
The re-thinking of preconceptions past:
Of what it means to be alive,
When it seems,
The purpose is but to strive,
To reach some imaginary mirage.
A trail of discarded lottery tickets
Leading to an endless, desperate marketing collage,
The essential entourage
Of all the cool stuff we're gonna need
When *Happiness* is the label's camouflage.
So, into an endless video reel of a voiceless, thoughtless montage.
Played under our chosen ironic soundtrack whose long forgotten, wholesome lyrics cannot be heard
Above the chattering, shredding,
Of five year plans forlorn, forecast,   cont.

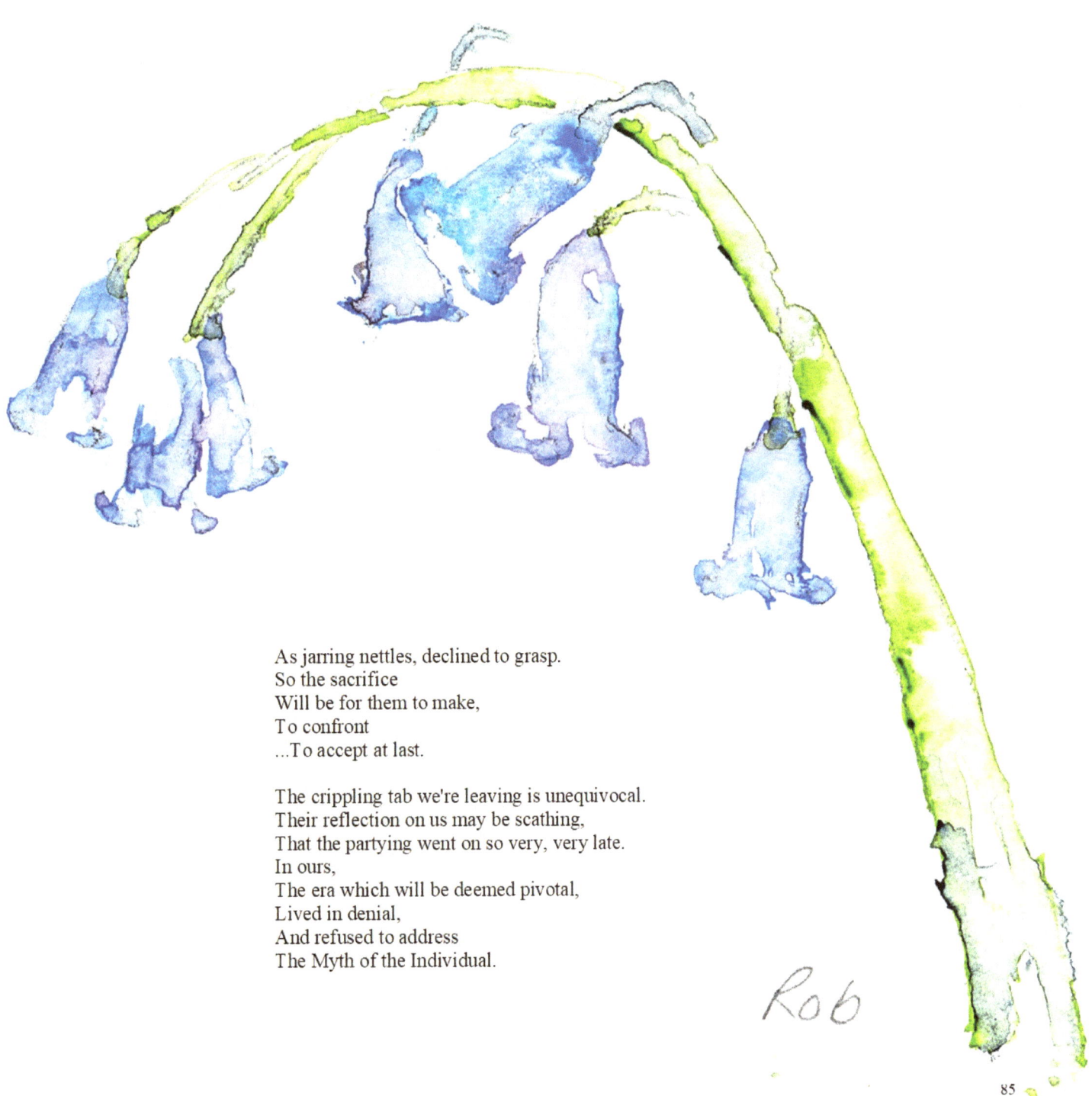

As jarring nettles, declined to grasp.
So the sacrifice
Will be for them to make,
To confront
...To accept at last.

The crippling tab we're leaving is unequivocal.
Their reflection on us may be scathing,
That the partying went on so very, very late.
In ours,
The era which will be deemed pivotal,
Lived in denial,
And refused to address
The Myth of the Individual.

Rob Kersley

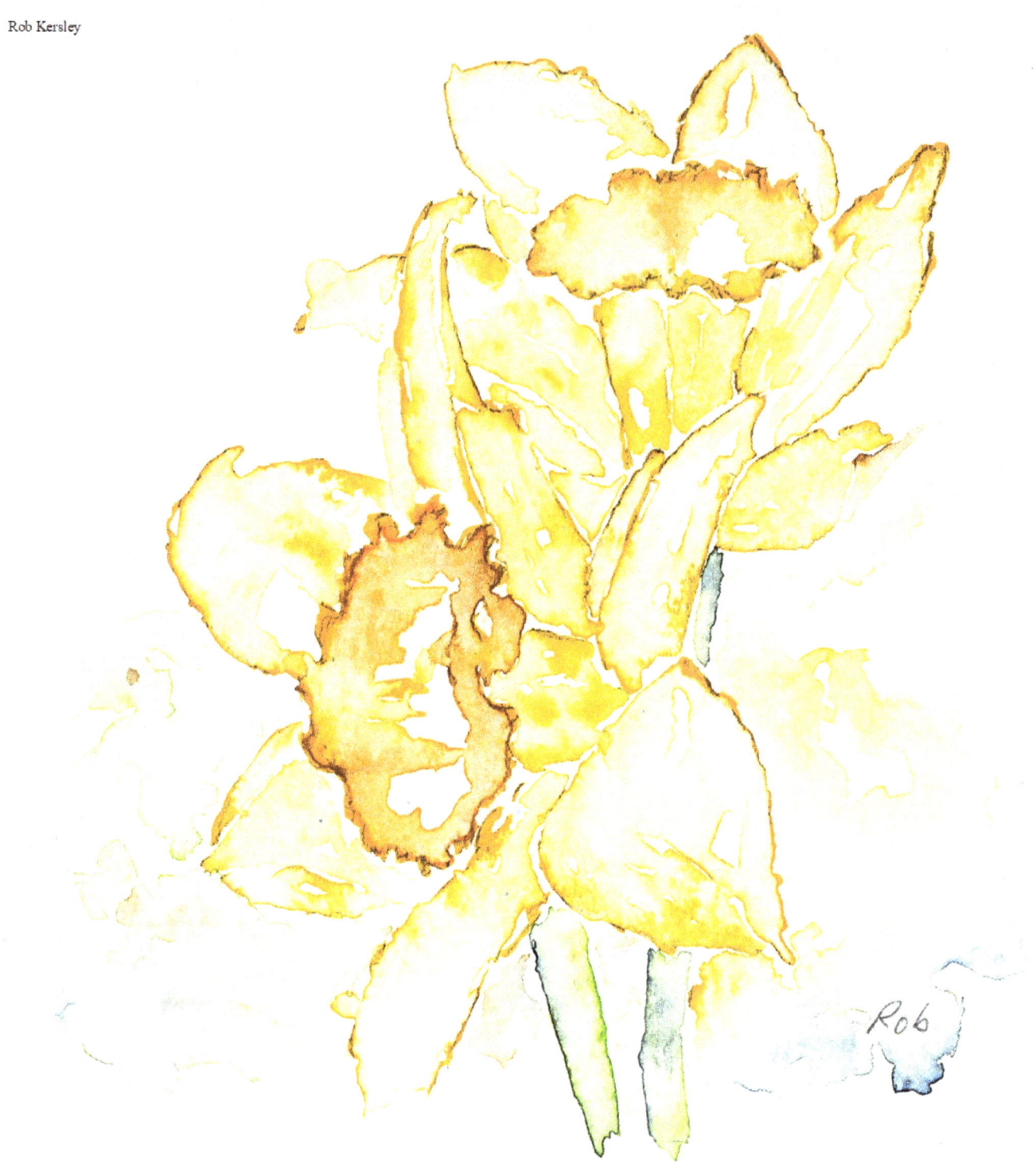

Evolve

Cardigan-sleeved hands fly up like a flume, in a
Carbon free, state of the art, paperless classroom,
Where floor to ceiling glass walls and table tops enable transparent illumination
For eager infants who swipe and tap their touch screen desks,
To find the history page in question.
Archive video of famine inset
With historical data on former Third World debt.
Simplified, bullet-point rows
And rolling, overlaid graphics that shows
The virtual elimination of emissions,
And the monumental efforts,
The last ditch desperation,
In the ongoing restoration
Of protective ozone insulation.

Educational newsreel images of the inevitable eruption,
Of international riots that finally put to bed
The curse of discrimination,
Followed by legal text of what,
For some years now, can never again be done or said.
Maps of familiar coastlines of continents, reproved,
Recognized only by their general outline,
All land borders long since removed.

The teacher points to one hand. The others are lowered.
And all eyes alight
On the studious but slight
Figure with short, dark hair,
For she can recite
The facts and cite
The dates and toll of the Great Pandemic.
But after twenty minutes recessed,
The teacher asks the class to attest
As to what had to be dispelled before any of these global issues could be properly addressed.

For to evolve is to suffer.
Evolution is painful effort.
Not to become a choir of uniformed, blank ciphers, chanting the same notes as their nearest,
Nor tied to the past, and a collection of egos behind their old boundaries
Singing their anthems of self-interest.   cont.

But what, in the centuries before would have defied convention
When, some might say we were too comfortable,
...I'm not so sure.
Perhaps we were distracted
Just as that fly,
Trying to find its way out of my open window.
Curiously drawn to the beckoning, brilliant, bright light on the other side,
But lured back to its own frantic reflection
That it could only find
In the closed pane.
Perhaps only our guardian of absolute necessity then
Could prove to be
Our mother of re-invention.
To a future that will balance the celebration of the irrepressible,
Across its indivisible shelf
But critically, center all focus on the others, not the self.

Hope, is a seed that we pray we've sowed,
In a future rising
Somewhere beyond our polluted horizon:
The class, as one stand
And place a youthfully firm hand
On their neighbour's shoulder.
The brave new world, seamless and irresistible,
Chant their response:
"Dispel
The Myth of the Individual".

Just Tell Me the Truth

Tell me it's not just about money,
That what we were taught still applies.
And tell me I wasn't deluded,
That it wasn't a cunning disguise.

Tell me that we're making progress,
That we do as we read in those books.
And tell me the future is rosy,
That it's nothing as bad as it looks.

Just tell me truth, I can take it,
I'm not after clever replies.
And save us from this, cos we're dying
The slow death, of a thousand more lies.

Rob Kersley

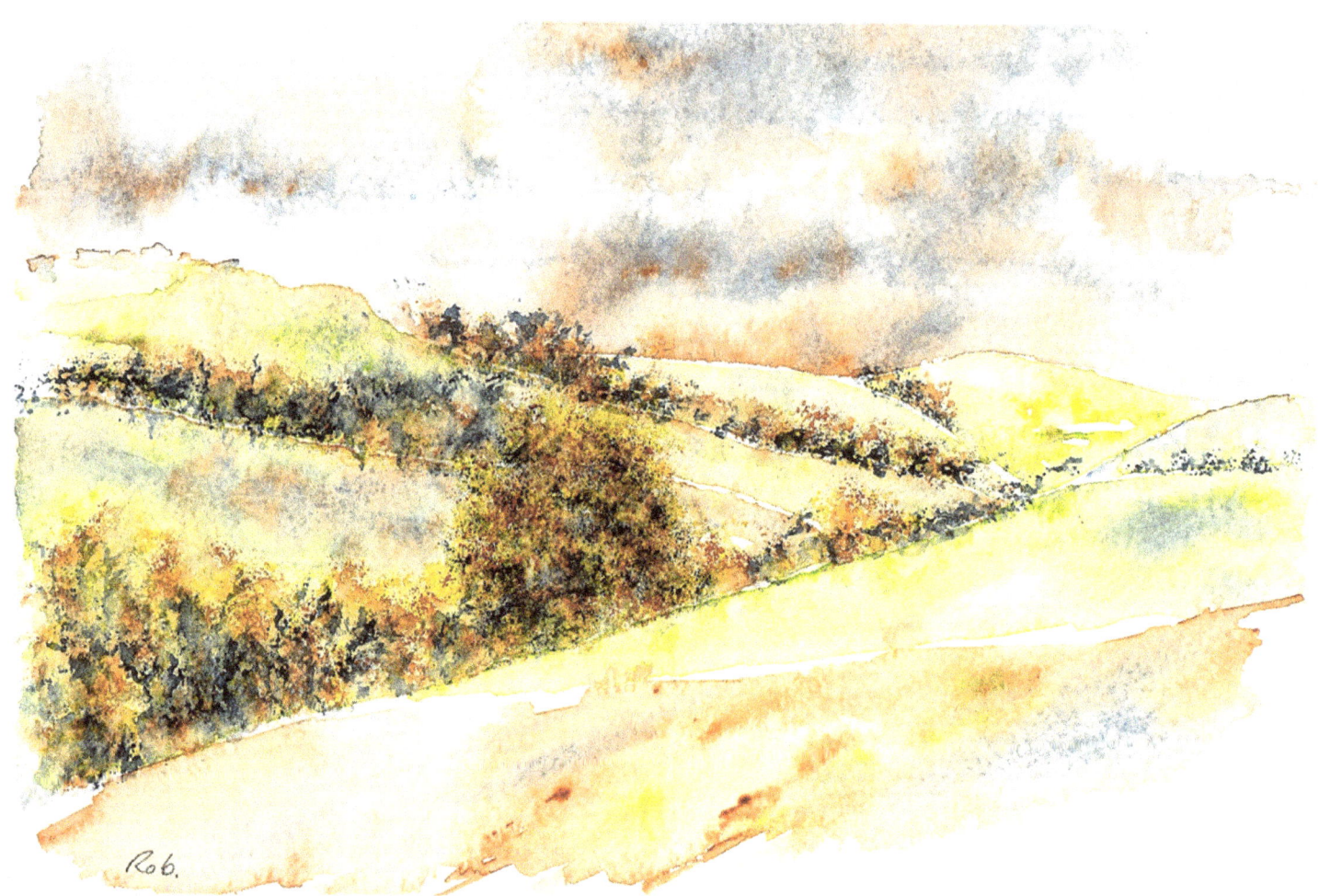

Feeling Thrown

Of bone, in stone,
Fired, glazed and prone.
Together, alone in feeling thrown...

Perhaps these days are meant to disorientate like this.
Perhaps the giddiness, the exhausting
Blur of events and vibrating din
Of conflicting tenets,
And this pressure,
Are but symptoms of the unrelenting efforts
To recenter us on our horizontally spinning wheels.

And when it pinches;
When it reaches
Way down
And squeezes
And draws so painfully outwards,
Forever, achingly upwards;
Then, perhaps this potter
Is creating, something
Even more beautiful
Than the imperfect clay,
We were getting used to.

Rob Kersley

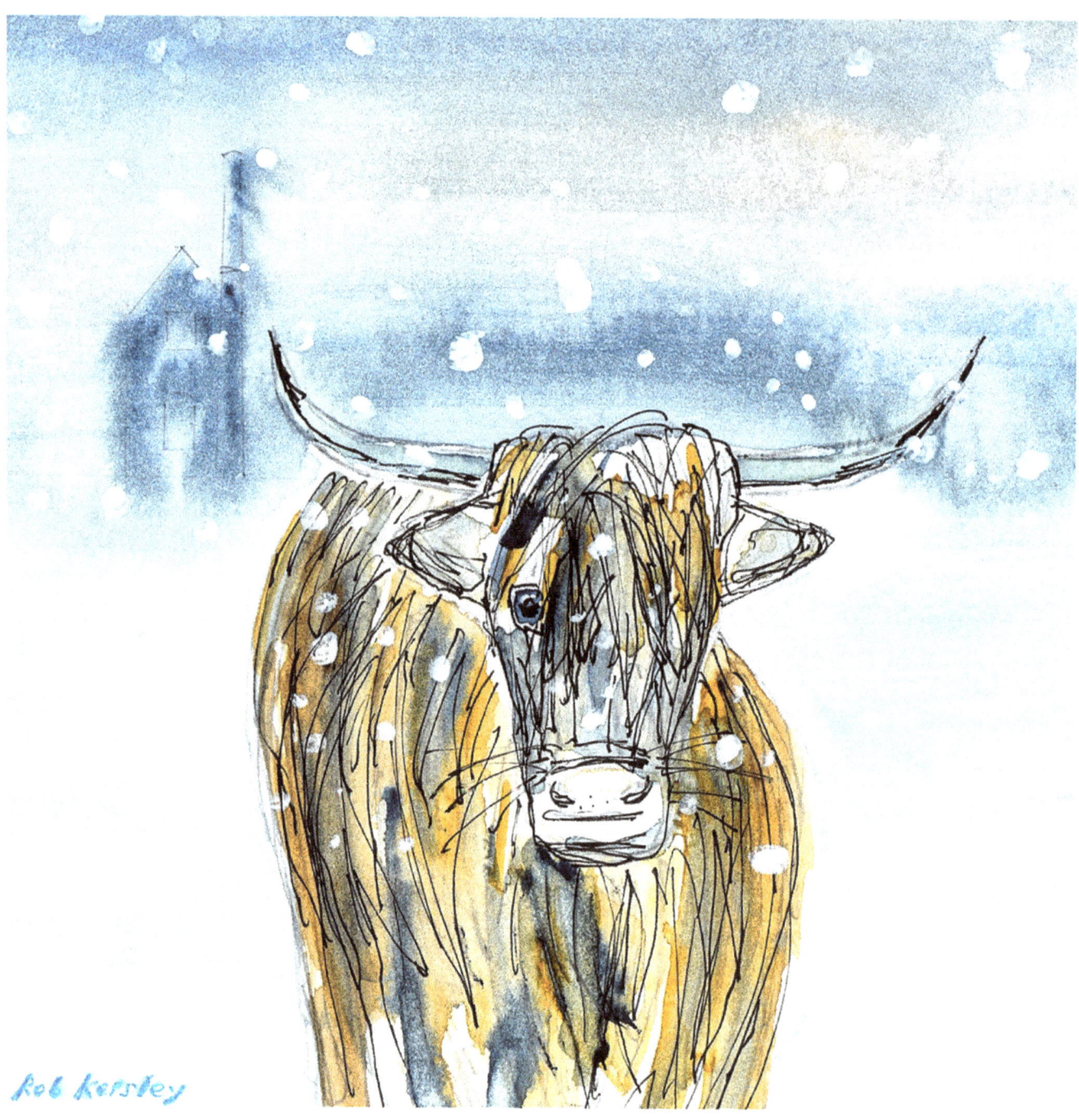

Homeward With Em' Spoonerisms

Tea tannin removed before we left,
So all our speans were glooming.

Through a Spanish night, one drove, one slept.
The mean shines bright, she's drooming.

Our CDs, left at home recessed,
So for all our teens, we're strooming.

Silves to St Just, first rain all year.
Typheens down 'ere, it's tooming!

Rob Kersley

Prime Location, Christmas Eve

There's a recessed doorway to the closed-down betting shop,
And oversized, grey paving slabs rise
A few degrees, so that it stays relatively dry.
And it's deep enough that when
Debbie and John and Luke and his dog lie
With their backs to the padlocked doors,
They can hardly be seen.

They can hardly be seen,
But if you stop, opposite the jewellers,
Turn away from the glinting gold
Ostentation encrusted watches,
Each competing for attention atop its box,
Like demigod badges,
To be paraded like trophies plundered in a zero-hour war
Bragging, while the brief spotlights locks.
Yes, if you dare
Look the other way, you will see
All four of them huddled, like day old pups there.

All four of them, huddled:
Luke's dog, a blend of Cardiff's strife and strays,
Watches over Luke with a loyalty that would shame a nation.
Luke and John take turns checking that
Debbie doesn't get drawn away
And goes the way
Of the friend she lost,
Whose damaged past and hunger cost
Her dear.

Her dear,
Dear friend was found near the bus station, sprawled like a rain soaked, crippled cat,
Enslaved between her terrifying neurosis, the bottle and the needle.
Anything to numb
The nineteen years of successive abusers,
That left her to conclude that she was to blame.
When routine violence, the whiskey and methadone confuses,
Her reality slid.
She prayed for the end
Which found her, four and half minutes before the ambulance did.   cont.

Before the ambulance did,
Debbie went for help.
She'd tugged at the sleeves of shoppers
Whom had problems of their own.
What with Marks running out of crackers for pity's sake
And the Waitrose delivery with more alternative items
Than a host that can boast fifteen for Christmas Day can be expected to cope
With. Quite enough stress thank you very much,
Without this random, wailing, clawing, swearing, pleading, homeless person,
Tugging at the sleeve of her nearly new coat.
Most distressing, it really was.

It really was, most distressing!
You'd think the authorities would have cleaned this place up.
After all, it's their choice if they want to be homeless.
They chose to be where they are.

They did choose to be where they are,
But choice it seems is a relative term.
For a ten foot doorway on Queen Street,
Is a relative prime location
For the four of them.
And you can see that they know they are in a relatively good place;
Luke is laughing, a skeletal version of his former self,
Gesturing, recounting something.
The empty hand sanitizer lies on its side,
An ironic reminder. Cider on breath, bottle on lap,
He's rambling from beneath
His old NY cap.
The others aren't sure where he's going with this and neither is Luke,
But they try their best, so they're smiling too.

They try their best
Because Christmas
Is for caring,
So,
That's what these four will do.

Nellie the President

Many Americans backed their Trump to send him back with a purpose,
But off he went like a tangerine schlump,
Trump! Trump! Trump!
Many Americans backed the lump who'd said, "...to Hell with the climate!",
And off he went to the gasoline dump,
Trump! Trump! Trump!
The rest of the world was calling,
Far, far away
Cos he'd said goodbye to the human rights of their people black or gay.
Though many Americans backed their Trump, who would let them all die from the virus,
He's denying his fate, but indictments await !!
Trump! ...Trump! ...Trump!

Rob Kersley

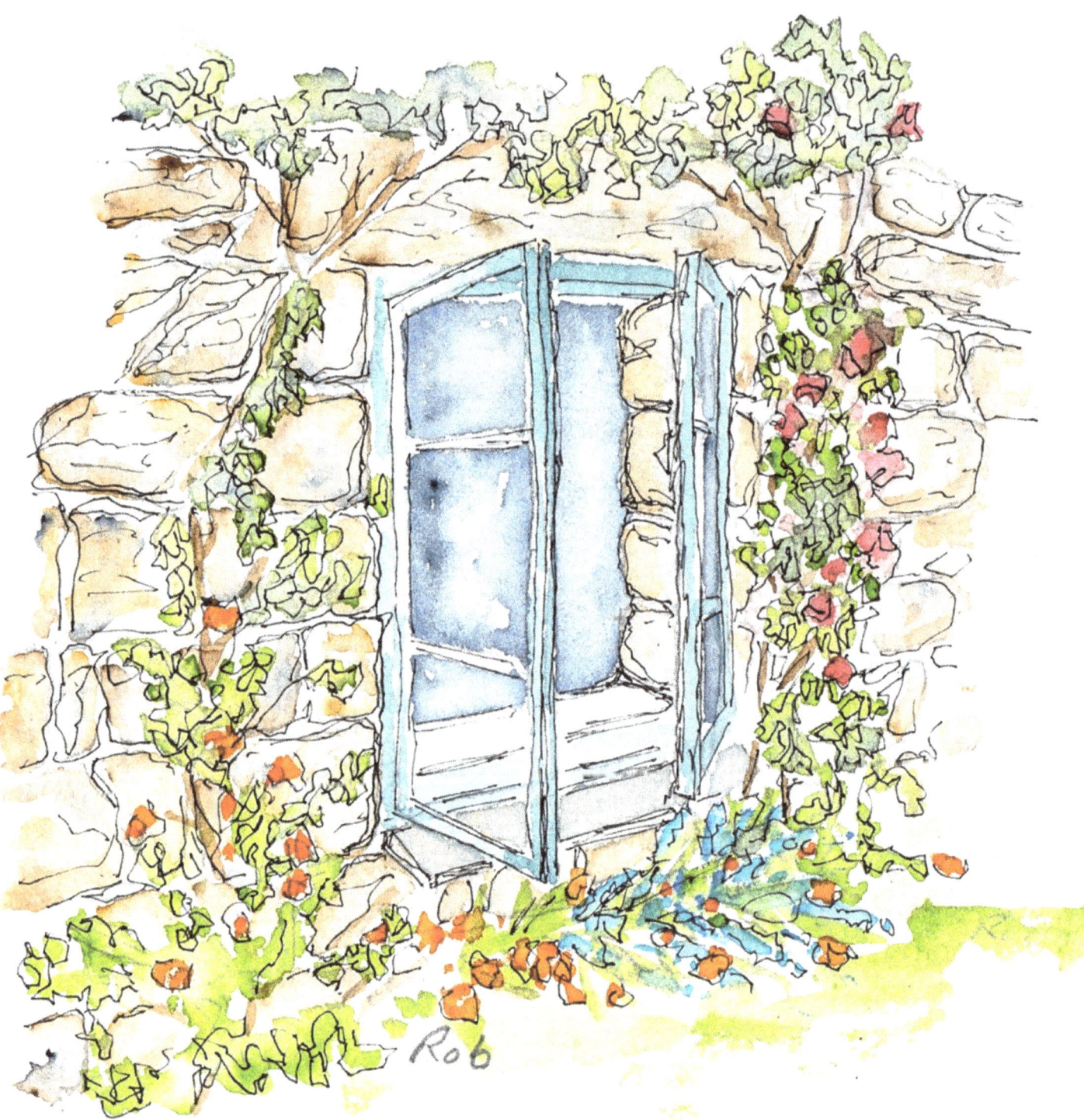

Look Inside

Look inside,
When all you see out there divides
To conquer. Mystified.

Look inside,
And open memories of clearer days;
Of lighter moods, like rays
Of warm sunshine on your smiling face.
When dark history was but a trace.
Before our leaders fell once more from grace.

Look inside,
And know,
The pains that glow, are how we grow.
And aching limbs and sad fatigue
Builds stronger souls tomorrow.

Look inside
With open heart,
And mind to reboot empathy.
For why, Ode to Joy
Was rejected,
As an anthem of peace and unity.

Look inside
The pages of twelve months past:
Sharp and shocking,
Socially distant, stopping
Progress here.
But awareness, sharpened by twenty-twenty vision,
Will help prepare us
For a whole New Year.

Rob.

ps:
Happy New Year!
...And may you look inside your jeans, to find them sufficiently elasticated to hurdle the challenges ahead!

Rob Kersley

Ten

From a month of fives and sixes,
Last Tuesday suddenly became a three.
I don't know why,
But the grey isolation found me
Missing everything,
Finding nothing here.
Over a year
Since we hugged family,
Too long since meeting friends.
And then,
Someone on the radio
With an accent so familiar,
Sent me back to a life lost.
In the wrong frame of mind,
A line seemingly crossed.
So Wednesday was a two.

Thursday might have been okay.
In spite of the horizontal rain,
The wild, whistling, whining wind,
It could have got to four again.
But my longing for normality,
Reminisced and missed its target
Of Sennen or Porthcurno
In late May.
It should have settled on this mystical coastline,
Anywhere from Gwynver to Hayle,
But I landed in a different time and place.
Still hearing that soft, sweet accent of home,
I could see the Honddu Valley.
I could actually hear its sibling river,
Smell the tall grass and its sun-bleached husk.
Dragon flies skimming the ripples at dusk
As it makes its timeless way from Sennybridge,
Down through Usk.

So Thursday was a nought,
And walls too wet to climb out,
A whole weekend of noughts followed.
Wales had won a game they tried very hard to lose,   cont.

I kept myself distanced from the infected, maskless news.
But four days of noughts laid waste,
As surely as the emptying of the heavens on this
Windswept, rain-soaked place.

But this morning,
Sunlight woke us as it rose just higher than before above Sancreed.
A six perhaps, but there was more.
A blackbird out of nowhere,
Broke the silence
With its thrilling singing;
Over spilling, like its little heart couldn't believe the brightness either,
Perfect stillness held the sunny morn.

The sunshine found our first daffodil,
My search to still
A longing for home, the longing for certainty, familiarity.
As certain as the birdsong I could now hear with growing clarity
Today was a ten,
Thanks to that blackbird and whomever settled him outside my window.
Today was a ten,
Thanks to the sunshine that broke through and lit your eyes like I remember them,
When we watched the rising tide kiss the bare prints we'd trod.

Today was a perfect ten, at last.
Today was at least a ten, thank God.

The England Machine

...(I sent this poem to the WRU Management who then posted it on the team notice board for motivation before the game. So if Alun Wyn Jones gets red-carded straight from the kick off, I take full responsibility!)

The England Machine comes to Wales,
The recurring old menace we face.
The arrival of our masters on Cardiff's wet streets,
To put Welsh identity back in its place.

The England Machine, like a galleon,
Whose lumbering hull heaves and lowers.
Reimagining past days of imperial crusades,
Its good folk, the brow-beaten rowers.

The England Machine closed our coal mines,
Then the England Machine sold our steel.
And then it pretends, with faint praise it extends,
A limp handshake on a servile deal.

The England Machine hates resistance,
'Cos the England Machine wants to own.
And its Establishment tells you, *"all men are born equal"*,
Especially the ones on the throne.

The England Machine seeks to trample,
With the flag of St George on its face.
But what the England Machine lacks in humility,
It makes up for in its absence of grace.

The England Machine will keep coming
To batter Welsh hearts 'til we fall
But the Welsh boys will do what the Welsh folk do best
Just keep getting back up,
To stand tall.

About the Author

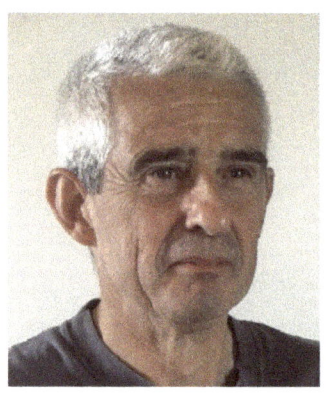

Rob Kersley was born in Usk, Wales and was educated at Wern Secondary Modern School and Mid-Gwent College, Pontypool. He worked as a carpenter/joiner, surveyor, manager, operations director and managing director before re-evaluating and re-training as a deep tissue therapist.

He then established himself as the sole practitioner of a well-respected and successful deep tissue therapy practice near Brecon from 2003 until 2018 before relocating with his wife Liz to Cornwall where his daughter had settled some years earlier.

He joined Coast FM in Penzance as a presenter in 2019 where he hosts a weekly radio show covering non-mainstream, contemporary artists and their music from around the globe. His poetry was first published in 2022, in version eight of Penny Authors. Having those poems published and seeing his work in print, woke an aspiration to publish his own books of art and poetry. This opportunity presented itself through Penny Authors, to fulfil a lifelong dream. This he seized, and this book is the first of many more to come.

www.ingramcontent.com/pod-product-compliance
Lightning Source LLC
Chambersburg PA
CBHW040543220526
45473CB00016B/3007